The Pearl

II

Paul's Primers—Book 1

The Pearl

The Captivating Story of the Wondrous Love of God

Paul Rakowicz

CJR Press
Highland, Michigan

IV

Copyright Information

Published by:
CJR Press
2255 Horseshoe Drive
Second Floor
Highland, MI 48356
info@cjrpress.com

Cover Design by Leann Pickard
Editing by CJR Press
Layout by CJR Press

International Standard Book Number (ISBN): 978-0-578-01723-5
Printed in the United States of America

Publish Date: 9/5/2017 A.D.
A.D. is "Anno Domini"
A.D. means "in the Year of our Lord"

Dedication

to my children
from whom I have learned the true depth of God's love

VIII

Table of Contents

X

Foreword

Trying to describe the beauty and glory of God in Christ, and the wonder of God's plan of salvation, is the colossal but compelling task Paul Rakowicz has undertaken. His passion is born of gratitude to God for what he calls "The Indestructible Way" earned by Christ and sealed to every believer. With all that is in him, Paul wants his readers to know the joy of God's fellowship through Christ. This is his dominating purpose for writing.

In a day when postmodern readers clamor for self-help, self-actualization, "have your best life now" materials, he dares to approach timeless topics that link our souls with God and eternity. He writes theology with conviction and imagination, often pushing the theological edge in making deductions or drawing inferences from Scripture to make a fuller picture of God's acts of Creation, the Fall of Man, and The Indestructible Way. He is not, however, interested in novelty but in the ancient truth as handed down from the Early Church Fathers, of whom St. John Chrysostom (c. A.D. 347–407, archbishop of Constantinople) is his favorite.

I join Paul in his hope that the Spirit of Christ will use his retelling of the foundational and eternal truths of the Bible to draw your spirit in reverential awe and gratitude to God to say, "What wondrous love is this!"

Dr. James N. McGuire, Senior Pastor Fellowship Presbyterian Church Livonia, Michigan

Dr. McGuire is an RTS (Reformed Theological Seminary) alumnus, and also holds degrees from Belhaven College in Jackson, Mississippi, and McCormick Theological Seminary. He served as the founding pastor of Lakeside Presbyterian Church from 1973–1995.

Acknowledgments

First, I want to acknowledge my lovely wife Carolyn, who passed from this earthly life into Heaven on June 7, 2017. She was a true Christian woman, wife and mother, whose simple faith remains an ongoing inspiration.

Then, our five children—Jessica, Cara, John, Caitlin, and Joline, all of whom supported me greatly during the original writing of this book. Without the prodding and encouragement from both my wife and children, I would never have embarked on this book, let alone been able to see it through to the end.

I also want to acknowledge the enduring influence of my father Chester (who passed from this earthly life into Heaven many years ago on September 14, 1981), and the continuing support and influence of my mother Rita. Many thanks are also due my friends, Dennis and Pat, for their advice and encouragement.

Finally—but always first in heart and mind—I want to thank Jesus Christ, by whom all things are possible.

4   The Pearl

Preface

Welcome to Paul's Primers. This series is intended to provide Christians, in as engaging a manner as possible, a means by which to understand their Christian faith more deeply and intimately than ever before. This series will provide answers to questions about some of the most important issues surrounding Christianity—answers that I hope and trust the reader will find credible, verifiable, reliable, believable, and, in the end, meaningful —even beyond the bounds of time. We will creatively present to you these Christian teachings from a *triumphant* viewpoint, such that you will find yourself coming to a better, and more positive and optimistic understanding, of these eternal truths. This will then enable you to live a more powerful and victorious Christian life.

Many years ago, the study of the Bible became the core mission of my life. I read the Bible over and over. I read the New Testament over and over. I read every translation of the New Testament I could get my hands on—including the original English version by William Tyndale for which he was eventually burned at the stake in 1536—ultimately even compiling my own easy-to-read and easy-to-understand version that our family uses yet today.

I studied the many and varied Christian denominations. I studied early church history. I studied the flow of cultures throughout the ages. Then, I began to piece together the story of the gospel message for the benefit and understanding of my wife and children.

I took the good from the church, I took the good from history, I took the good from the church's ongoing fragmentation (taking the good from each of the many different denominations), and I pieced it all together. As a born teacher and "clarifier," I sought the simple elegance evident in all real truth, and pieced together the "best-of-the-best" from all of my studies.

What I found was amazing—I found that the gospel of Jesus Christ was the single most compelling story I had ever come across. This first book in the Paul's Primers series is the culmination of the tale that unfolded before my very eyes as a result of my search. This tale, this presentation of the gospel of Jesus Christ, so captivated my wife and children that they encouraged me to share this presentation of the Kingdom with others. Thus was born the Paul's Primers series. I hope you will benefit from my journey, and that this presentation of the gospel of the Kingdom will captivate you and your family as it has ours.

Now, given the nature of this subject matter—eternal Christendom, and that life *beyond* the bounds of time available to all its citizens—it is purposely written in a somewhat "proper" and "formal" manner. I believe this is appropriate to the magnitude and grandeur of the subject. It is not, by any means, inaccessible or beyond the scope and reach of the average reader. It was, and is, as a primer series, simply meant to share the grandeur of the subject matter *and*, at the same time, allow the reader opportunity to elevate their minds to the level of the subject's majesty and glory.

With this style of writing, and given the subject matter, you may periodically come across words or ideas that are new to you. If this happens, please don't be alarmed. You will find that I will often provide a simple and readily understandable definition or explanation of the word or idea alongside it, or in the Glossary. You will also often see the word or idea used throughout the paragraph to help you understand the context in which the word or idea is used in Christian teaching.

With this said, it is important to keep in mind that during the Preface, Introduction, and Overview, I am introducing topics only in summary form. Therefore, if any of these topics are new to you and you find I do not explain them thoroughly enough in these early sections— again, don't be alarmed. As you read further into the book, you will see that these concepts are more fully developed—often many different times, as we progress deeper and deeper into the creation account.

In the end, regardless of your reading level or present "depth" of scholarly theological knowledge, the book is written as a primer ("a small introductory book on a subject—a short informative piece of writing"—see Glossary), meant to offer you great benefit, regardless of your current level of Christian understanding. It provides helpful and meaningful information on many levels, from the beginner on up.

If you think, or maybe were taught, that the depth of the revealed word is not for the "average" person, I ask that you consider rethinking your position, for I submit to you that the revelation of God is for any and all who will simply *come* to the living Word. Even back when Jesus walked the earth, it is evident that understanding came not based on educational backgrounds, but only to those willing to allow the Spirit to guide them into His truth. Both the scholar—the Apostle Paul, and the fisherman—the Apostle Peter, were equally able to come to know the depth of the wonder of the living God ("When they saw the complete assurance of Peter and John, who were obviously uneducated and untrained men, they were staggered." [Acts 4:13 Phillips]).

Today, if *you* are of a willing spirit, this same Spirit will lead *you* into the depth of all truth. "For this is the covenant that I will make with the House of Israel: After those days, says the Lord, I will put My laws in their mind and write them on their hearts; and I will be their God, and they shall be My people. None of them shall teach his fellow-citizen, and none his brother, saying, 'Know the Lord,' for all shall know Me, from the least to the greatest of them. For I will be merciful to their unrighteousness, and their sins and their lawless deeds I will remember no more." (Heb 8:10–12 Phillips-ed. PBR)

And know that you, as a Christian, are indeed to whom the Lord here speaks, for it is to all the citizens of Christendom that He says: " … you are God's 'chosen race,' His 'royal priesthood,' His 'holy nation,' His 'peculiar people'—all the old titles of God's people now belong to you. It is for you now to demonstrate the goodness of Him who has called you out of darkness into His marvelous light. In the past you were not 'a people' at all: but now you are the people of God! In the past you had no experience of His mercy, but now it is intimately yours!" (1 Pet 2:9–10 Phillips-ed. PBR)

So have no fear as you proceed—as a Christian you were created and formed to intimately know God; you were literally built for this very purpose! No matter how deep the theological issue, your mind is created in such a way that it can readily apprehend the eternal truths of Christianity. There is *no* essential Christian doctrine that is beyond your personal understanding, regardless of your educational background in this material world ("But the Comforter, which is the Holy Spirit, whom the Father will send in my Name, He shall teach you all things, and bring all things to your remembrance, which I have told you." [Jn 14:26 GNV-ed. PBR]).

The Lord is gracious, and has created all of His people, (even you!) in His very own image; therefore His word is that which is natural to your very being.

As for material covered in this primer series, you will find that in Book One, the focus is on the three main characters of eternal Christendom—the created angels, the uncreated Jesus Christ, and created mankind—all through a study of the initial hours and days of the creation account as found in the first three chapters of Genesis. One might say that Book One presents, for the reader in search of fine pearls, that one pearl of great price, the Gospel of Jesus Christ in its earliest and most fundamental form—as it existed in the time before time, even *before* the foundation of the world!

However, before you embark on the journey this first book offers, I ask that you, in keeping with the goal of elevating the mind to the majesty and glory of the subject matter, take a moment to contemplate the following quote from Johann Wolfgang von Goethe, as recorded less than two weeks before his death. Personally, I find taking such a moment invaluable in helping me truly appreciate the very real, and intimate, presence of the living God, our Lord and Savior Jesus Christ:

> "Beyond the grandeur and the moral elevation of
> Christianity, *as it sparkles and shines in the Gospels,*
> the human mind will not advance."
> (italics in the original)[1]

To my way of thinking, such words as these are hard to improve upon. For in truth, the teachings of Jesus Christ, as found in the Gospels and throughout the New Testament, are the most sublime (see Glossary) of all creation—and history—and above all of the knowledge known to man!

I also want to point out that these teachings of our Lord Jesus Christ, as they sparkle and shine in the Gospels and throughout the New Testament, rest easily upon their foundation, the Old Testament Scriptures, which speak often of the Christ, just as Christ spoke often and easily from and about them.

In truth, what we find is that the Old Testament Scriptures are, in fact, a part of the Christian Gospel of Jesus Christ. Every Old Testament saint now living in Heaven with Jesus in the communion of the saints, was indeed a Christian—even while living on this earth before the physical advent of the Christ ("Your father Abraham rejoiced to see my *(Jesus')* day, and he saw it, and was glad." [Jn 8:56 GNV-ed. PBR] "Men and brethren, I can surely speak freely to you about the patriarch David ... He foresaw the resurrection of Christ, and it is this of which he is speaking when he said that His soul was not left in Hell, neither His flesh did see corruption." [Acts 2:29–31 Phillips-ed. PBR]).

Jesus Christ and His Gospel message "The Kingdom of God!" are the heart and soul and the very essence and purpose of every single solitary word found in the Old Testament. The New Testament sits as the crown jewel upon the Old, even upon the whole of the completed revelation of God to man. There is not now, nor has there ever been, nor will there ever be for this present world, words and teachings beyond the grandeur and moral elevation of this fully revealed Christianity.

Now these biblical teachings of our Lord Jesus Christ are nobility in action (of mind, body, and spirit) and the great calling of all those living as citizens of eternal Christendom. This call of noble purpose shines forth in the life of our Christian forefathers. It started with the very first Christians—Adam and Eve—who became believers in the Christ and thus Christians at His first recorded prophetic proclamation in Genesis 3:15, and proceeded through Abel, and Enoch, and Noah, and Abraham, and Moses, and David, and Elijah—along with so many others—and finally through Jesus and the Apostles.

Further, this very Bible, which we also refer to as Scripture, not only presents our noble calling but also provides the knowledge, through its sublime teachings, of the means by which to attain this calling. Finally, in this Bible (the authoritative record of the Word of the Living God, consisting of the books of the New Testament as commonly received, along with the books of the Old Testament as found in the Septuagint and Hebrew texts) we find, ultimately, from beginning to end, from Alpha to Omega (see Rv 21:6), the story of Christianity and eternal Christendom.

Now when we as Christians read Scripture, be it Old or New Testament—for it is all one Christ given Gospel of the Kingdom of God, we find ourselves reading it with the "veil" lifted, for as Christians, the veil has actually been lifted by Christ.

What we mean by this is simple. You see, with our belief in the resurrected and ascended (that is to say, "lifted") physical body of the Christ—which is the veil (see Heb 10:19–20)—the mystery of the faith is revealed. Therefore, when reading the Bible, even when reading the Old Testament of this Word of the Living God, it is impossible for us to read it without seeing Jesus Christ on every page. Did not even Jesus teach us as such? " ... Behold, I *(Jesus)* have come—in the volume of the book it is written of me ....." (Heb 10:7 Phillips-ed. PBR)

When reading the New Testament of this Word of the Living God, not only do we see Jesus Christ on every page, but we also find what is referred to as the "historical" Jesus. And what we find as Christians for whom the veil has actually been lifted by Christ, is that this historical Jesus, who is the Christ, is literally God Incarnate ("Behold, a virgin shall be with child, and shall bear a son, and they shall call His name Emmanuel, which is by interpretation, God with us." [Mt 1:23 GNV-ed. PBR])—that which is God making up the person, the flesh and blood in which God became Incarnate, making up the man.

What we also discover is that any attempt to understand this Jesus only as a man, and not as what He truly was— the living God transcending time and space through the Incarnation—causes us to lose all perspective, and, thus, we completely fail in any attempt to come to know this God. How fatal it is to lose perspective in this way! For this Jesus is the main character throughout the whole of Scripture!

You may now be asking yourself, "How is it that Jesus Christ is the main character of the *entire* Bible?" The answer is both simple and astounding—for this Jesus of the New Testament is the very One of the Old Testament by whom the universe was brought into existence! "Now Christ is the visible expression of the invisible God. He is the firstborn of all created things, for by Him all things were made, that are in heaven, and that are in earth, seen or unseen. Through Him, and for Him, also, were created power and dominion, ownership and authority. In fact, every single thing was created through and for Him. He is both the first principle and the upholding principle of the whole scheme of creation. And now He is the head of the body which is composed of all Christian people. Life from nothing began through Him, and life from the dead began through Him; therefore, He is justly called the Lord of all. It was in Him that the full nature of God chose to live, and through Him, God planned to reconcile in His own person, as it were, everything on earth and everything in Heaven by virtue of the sacrifice of the cross." (Col 1:15–20 Phillips-ed. PBR)

Therefore, when we, as Christians, read our Bibles, we do so with the veil already lifted by Christ. Through this crystal clear view, we come to understand that indeed Christianity did not begin with Matthew 1:1, but instead eternally exists. Jesus Christ, the one and only true God, the God of the one and only *truly* royal faith, is the One who "in the beginning ... created the heaven and the earth." (Gn 1:1 LXX)

Now, before proceeding from this Preface on to the Introduction, let's take a brief moment to discuss the triune nature of God. You will find that while we speak often of Jesus Christ as the living God, we will also speak in terms of the triune "nature" of God. This is because our profession of faith includes the understanding that God exists in three persons—the Father, the Son, and the Holy Spirit—while also including the understanding that though there are these three, there is yet only one God.

Thus we are monotheists, who believe that while this one true and living God eternally exists as three persons, Jesus Christ is the focal point of our worship, for He alone " … is the visible expression of the invisible God … " (Col 1:15 Phillips) " … the image of the invisible God … " (Col 1:15 KJV).

This understanding is vital, for this understanding provides the *only* means by which we can understand the *one* true and living God. For, you see, there are many who claim to worship a "God the Father"—but who do not believe that their version of god the father became manifest unto mankind as Jesus Christ. There are many who claim to worship a "Spirit" or a "great Spirit"—but who do not believe that their spirit became manifest unto mankind as Jesus Christ. There are many who acknowledge there was one known as the "Son of God"—but who do not believe that their version of the son of god is indeed Emmanuel, God with us, the living triune God—incarnate as the Christ.

But we, as Christians, worship Jesus Christ alone, the single manifestation of the triune God we know as the Father, the Son, and the Holy Spirit. We profess that *only* through the worship of the Son, Jesus Christ, and acknowledging Him as the living God incarnate by whom all things were made, can one *truly* come to know the eternal God of heaven and earth.

Hear the words of our Lord Himself, as given us through John: "God has given you all a certain amount of spiritual insight, and indeed I have not written this warning as if I were writing to men who don't know what error is. I write because your eyes are clear enough to discern a lie when you come across it. And what, I ask you, is the crowning lie? Surely the denial that Jesus is the Christ. I say, therefore, that any man who refuses to acknowledge the Father and the Son is anti-Christ. The man who will not recognize the Son cannot possibly know the Father; yet the man who believes in the Son will find that he knows the Father as well.

"For yourselves I beg you to stick to the original teaching. If you do, you will be living in fellowship with both the Father and the Son. And that means sharing His own life forever, as He has promised." (1 Jn 2:20–25 Phillips-ed. PBR)

Thus, we will speak of God as did the Apostles, glorifying Jesus Christ as the only true and living God, while acknowledging the triune nature of the only true and living God whose "fullness" was in the human body of that Christ (see Col 2:9).

FOR REFERENCE, HERE IS THE LIST OF BOOKS THAT MAKE UP THE SCRIPTURES:

Old Testament—thirty-nine books: Genesis, Exodus, Leviticus, Numbers, Deuteronomy, Joshua, Judges, Ruth, Kings I (1 Samuel), Kings II (2 Samuel), Kings III (1Kings), Kings IV (2 Kings), Chronicles I, Chronicles II, Ezra, Nehemiah, Esther, Job, Psalms, Proverbs, Ecclesiastes, Song of Solomon, Isaiah, Jeremiah, Lamentations, Ezekiel, Daniel, Hosea, Joel, Amos, Obadiah, Jonah, Micah, Nahum, Habakkuk, Zephaniah, Haggai, Zechariah, Malachi.

Septuagint Apocryphal Deutero-Canonical—eleven books: I Esdras, Tobit, Judith, The Book of Wisdom, The Wisdom of the Son of Sirach (Ecclesiasticus), Baruch, Epistle of Jeremiah, I Maccabees, II Maccabees, III Maccabees, IV Maccabees. The following are included in the Septuagint Apocrypha though technically they are a considered in the Septuagint a part of other Old Testament books: Additions to Daniel—Song of the Three Children, Susanna, Bel and the Dragon. Additions to II Chronicles (specifically the penitential prayer to God of Manasseh, King of Judah, alluded to in II Chronicles 33:18)—Prayer of Manasseh.[2]

Hebrew Apocryphal Deutero-Canonical books as originally provided with the King James Translation: Tobit, Judith, Ester (Greek), Wisdom, Sirach Prolog, Sirach, Baruch, Epistle of Jeremiah, Prayer of Azariah, Susanna, Bel, I Maccabees, II Maccabees, 1 Esdras, Prayer of Manasseh, 4 Esdras.

New Testament—twenty-seven books—common order: Matthew, Mark, Luke, John, Acts, Romans, 1 Corinthians, 2 Corinthians, Galatians, Ephesians, Philippians, Colossians, 1 Thessalonians, 2 Thessalonians, 1 Timothy, 2 Timothy, Titus, Philemon, Hebrews, James, 1 Peter, 2 Peter, 1 John, 2 John, 3 John, Jude, Revelation.

New Testament—twenty-seven books—in approximate chronological order with approximate dates according to the work, *The Development of the New Testament* by Arthur M. Ogden:[3] I Thessalonians, late 52 AD; II Thessalonians, early 53 AD; Galatians, 55–56 AD; I Corinthians, spring of 57 AD; II Corinthians, autumn of 57 AD; Romans, early 58 AD; Matthew, between 55 & 63 AD; Mark, between 60 & 61 AD; Luke, between 57 & 62 AD; John, between 60 & 64 AD; James, 60–62 AD; Philippians, spring of 63 AD; Ephesians, summer of 63 AD; Colossians, summer of 63 AD; Philemon, summer of 63 AD; Acts, summer 63 AD; Hebrews, 63–64 AD; I Peter, spring / summer of 64 AD; Titus, spring / summer of 64 AD; I Timothy, late 64 / early 65 AD; II Peter, summer 65 AD; Jude, summer 65 AD; II Timothy, autumn of 65 AD; I John, late 64 / early 65 AD; II John, late 64 / early 65 AD; III John, late 64 / early 65 AD; Revelation, late 65 / early 66 AD by John.

Introduction

Christianity, the story of the Bible, has as its main character, Jesus Christ; and the story of Christendom goes all the way back to Genesis, Chapter One. In point of fact, eternal Christendom goes back even further than that. For before Genesis 1:1, in the time before time— referred to in Scripture as "before the foundation of the world," we find the *true* "beginnings" of Christianity.

Listen as the Word speaks to us of this time before time: "Father, I will that they also, whom thou hast given me, be with me where I am; that they may behold my glory, which thou hast given me: for thou lovedst me before the foundation of the world." (John 17:24 KJV)

In Ephesians, the Word teaches us that Christians were chosen in Christ even before time began: "According as He hath chosen us in Him before the foundation of the world, that we should be holy and without blame before Him in love." (Eph 1:4 KJV)

In First Peter, we see again that the Christ was foreordained in this time before time: "Who *(speaking of Christ)* verily was foreordained before the foundation of the world, but was manifest in these last times for you." (1 Pet 1:20 KJV)

Christendom "began" before Genesis 1:1, so we refer to the "beginning" of Christianity in quotes for, in truth, Christianity is eternal. As we have just seen above, Christianity, when viewed with the veil lifted, is present in the very Increate (meaning "uncreated—existing without having been created"—see Glossary) of the Universe— Christianity is a literal part of the very nature of God!

And we know that the Incarnate God Jesus Christ " ... is always the same, yesterday, today and forever." (Heb 13:8 Phillips) Christianity, therefore, like the Increate God, was never really created, it simply always existed.

In order to understand this eternal Christianity, we have to come to understand something of this time before time, and in so doing, we can then understand the very plan of God. And by understanding the very plan of God in the time before time, we can then understand the context of the creation itself.

Further, by understanding the very plan of God before the foundation of the world, we can also then come to understand free will, and its interplay amidst the events of creation. We speak here of the interplay of free will as it played itself out during the hours and days of the initial creation between the three major players in the story of Christianity: the created angels, the Increate God, and created mankind.

To begin, then, to understand something of this time before time, before even Genesis Chapter One and the foundation of the world, before there was anything at all of the material or spiritual creation, we need to understand that there was once but One alone—God. This One God was, as He is yet today, a Spirit. And this Spirit God, eternally existing as the Father, Son, and Holy Spirit, was that God who would become Incarnate as the Christ. Yes, this God, visibly manifested unto us as Jesus Christ, is the singular and unique Increate of the Universe.

And in this time before time, before the foundation of the world, when God alone existed, this triune God purposed a creation in which beings with free will could "choose" to fellowship with Him for all eternity. He simply desired a Kingdom in which beings chose of their own free will to live in harmony with Him.

In so doing, of course, He obviously recognized that creating such beings with said free will would mean a bit of chaos. It would mean that they could, and therefore some of them absolutely would, choose to disregard Him—and thus leave His fellowship. This is just the nature of "free will"—that some would stay and some would go. In fact, it would not be free will at all if no one ever chose to leave His fellowship.

And so this intentional desire of God to implement such a creation, complete with the necessary chaos that would naturally ensue, is the starting point for our understanding. Only with the veil lifted by Christ will we be able to understand the beautiful way (but oh so incredibly passionate, as it included of necessity the burden of the cross), in which the Increate God was able to foreordain a creation in which the interplay of free will between the three main characters of creation would be valid—while at the same time ensuring that those who chose eternal fellowship with Him would ultimately have indestructible access thereto.

Let's next move on to understanding something of the angels, who were created before mankind. We will learn more of the angels as we proceed, but for now, when considering the angels, it is important to understand that they were a created kind, which, from the very start, were of the metaphysical world. In God's plan for them, He did not include a remedy for any inevitable breach of protocol because of free will. There was but banishment in the metaphysical Tartarus, which was created just for this purpose.

Why, you may ask? For there was and is no blood in the metaphysical world, by which to obtain redemption. Recall the words of our Lord delivered to us in the Epistle to the Hebrews: " ... For without the shedding of blood, there is no forgiveness." (Heb 9:22 NLT)

Further, all the angels were created at once in their fully mature forms, and each one could choose whether to live in fellowship with their Creator, or be banished from His presence forever. This was a choice each would make of their own free will, once and only once, right around the time of the formation of Adam.

Finally, we need to understand something of mankind. What we will see as we proceed with this study is that in the Lord's plan for man, whom He created as the highest order of His creation, there was included a two-tier structure. This structure was so designed that it would allow not only for mankind's inevitable fall, as free-will beings, but also for their full and complete redemption as well.

As a part of this two-tier structure, God intended for mankind to ultimately reign with Him in Heaven, even over and above the angels who were created before them. We will later see how this carefully planned heavenly order formed the basis of angelic sin.

For now, though, let us look in more detail at these two tiers for mankind. Starting with the second tier, with the veil lifted by Christ, we can come to understand that it is indeed Paradise that was created on day one of creation, as a part of the Kingdom of Light, and exists yet today in the third heaven (we'll learn more about the third heaven, the Kingdom of Light, Paradise, and this second tier as we proceed into the creation account).

This Paradise is on a completely different and altogether higher plane than the material world. It is not in any particular direction such as "up" or "down," but instead is of a totally different type or kind. It is all around us, just of a different dimension. It is the place wherein the thief on the cross was with Jesus that Good Friday afternoon immediately after he died. Recall the conversation: "And he *(the thief)* said unto Jesus, 'Lord, remember me, when you come into[4] your Kingdom.' Then Jesus said unto him, 'Verily I say unto thee, today shalt thou be with me in Paradise.'" (Luke 23:42–43 GNV-ed. PBR)

So the second tier is a place not meant for these physical bodies we have in this material world, but instead, a place meant for us after our time on this earth is complete: "It is written, moreover, that: 'The first man, Adam, became a living soul' *(tier one)*; the last Adam a life-giving Spirit *(tier two)*. But we should notice that the order is 'natural' first *(tier one),* and then 'spiritual' *(tier two)*. The first man came out of the earth, a material creature *(tier one)*. The second man came out of Heaven *(tier two)*. For the life of this world *(tier one)*, men are made like the material man; but for the heavenly life *(tier two)*, they are made like the one from Heaven. Just as we have been made like the material pattern *(tier one)*, so we shall be made like the Heavenly pattern *(tier two)*. For I assure you, my brothers, it is utterly impossible for flesh and blood *(tier one)* to inherit the Kingdom of God *(tier two)*. The transitory corruptible body made of material of this earth could never inherit the everlasting, incorruptible nature of the non-material spirit world." (1 Cor 15:45–50 Phillips-ed. PBR)

And what is the first tier? Why, it is the whole of the material creation! For the truth is quite simply this, that all of the material creation was made for one single purpose— that the "heirs of salvation" endowed with free will might ultimately have an indestructible Way into Paradise, the result of which includes the full resolution of the mutinous interplay of free will.

Then, through the installation of this indestructible Way into Paradise, the natural flow of procreation would provide, generation after generation, the never-ending increase of the Kingdom ("One generation passeth away, and another generation cometh: but the earth abideth forever." [Eccl 1:4 KJV-ed. PBR] "Of the increase of His government and peace there shall be no end ...." [Is 9:7 KJV]).

And this never-ending increase of the Kingdom of God is why mankind, unlike angel kind, was formed not all at once in their full numbers, but instead as "Adam," that through procreation the seemingly unending generations have, and continue now, to come forth.

Overview

Here it is, 2009 *Anno Domini Nostri Jesu Christi* (In the Year of Our Lord Jesus Christ), some two thousand years after the implementation of the indestructible Way. Almost ten thousand years after Genesis 1:1 and the actual creation. And the greatest topic of our time remains this creation and its creator, Jesus Christ.

In this book, we will embark on a study of this very subject. We will study God's plan before the foundation of the world; the implementation of that plan through the glorious creation of the heaven and the earth; and the impact of that plan upon the angels and mankind, both through the generations, and in our present lives.

But before we do that, let us first review the end of the story up to and including the Ascension; specifically how the Lord God resolved free will within the context of creation and implemented the indestructible Way such that, through the natural flow of procreation, the never-ending increase of the Kingdom of Jesus Christ could eternally proceed. Only with this knowledge can we then, in its proper context and with the veil lifted, read and come to understand the creation and its inherent crisis of choice.

Let's begin by imagining, if you will, the Increate God, triune in nature and visibly manifest unto us as Jesus Christ; this God Almighty who spoke to Abraham; the great "I AM" who spoke to Moses at Mount Sinai, and the people of the first century throughout Galilee and in Jerusalem; the creator of all things, by whose being and word all things exist and are upheld. Imagine this incredible creator God who has no beginning and no end, who is eternal, omniscient, omnipotent, and omnipresent. Imagine Him, the great Increate of the Universe, planning, in the time before time, the humbling of Himself to become one of us, one of His own creation. Why would He do such a thing?

Further, imagine this great Increate of the Universe— visibly manifest unto us as Jesus Christ, the Son sent by the Father, literally the Word of the Father made flesh — subjecting Himself to death on a cross, and not only to death on a cross but to a death brought about by the rejection of Him by the very beings that He Himself created! Murdered by His own creation!

Can there be a cup more bitter? Can there be any greater disgrace? And yet, somehow, we see that " … He Himself endured a cross and thought nothing of its shame …." (Heb 12:2 Phillips)

But why? Why would He do such a thing? Why would He subject Himself to such a fate? Why would Jesus agree to be " … the author and finisher of our faith …?" (Heb 12:2 Phillips-ed. PBR) Why would He create things so?

" … Because of the joy He knew would follow His suffering; and He is now seated at the right hand of the throne of God." (Heb 12:2 Phillips-ed. PBR)

And what is He speaking of here? What joy? What suffering?

Well, the suffering part we know well, for who among us has not heard of the birth of the Son of God through the miraculous Incarnation, of His teaching, of His miracles, of His healings, and finally, of His passion on the cross? Who among us has not heard tell of the pain and suffering He endured on our behalf on that old wooden cross?

But joy followed.

What was the basis of that joy? Was it not how the Lamb of God, in the Spirit as that Lion of the tribe of Juda, immediately after leaving the cross that Good Friday afternoon, triumphantly descended into Hell, and upon His arrival, broke down its gates and called forth the captive saints through His preaching?

And did He not then prove this joyous victory through His demonstration of power as He literally raised His body from the grave? ("Jesus answered and said unto them, 'Destroy this temple, and in three days I will raise it up.'" [Jn 2:19 KJV-ed. PBR])

And finally, in that risen body, He crossed over into Heaven at the glorious Ascension! Was this not the basis of the joy that followed?

But then what *was* the joy that followed?

The joy that followed was the full and final implementation of the indestructible Way, the freeing of mankind from the horror of being held captive by the prince of darkness, the resolution of mutinous free will within the creation, and the enabling of the never-ending growth of the Kingdom of God: literally—the reconciliation of the world! This was the joy of which He spoke.

Now all of this was all brought about by the suffering and subsequent triumph of the Christ. When you think about it, using the incarnation, teaching, miracles, healings, passion, and triumphant descent into Hell, with subsequent resurrection and ascension, was the *only* way in which the Increate God could create beings with real free will and, at the same time, create an indestructible Way unto Heaven.

Remember that, by definition, free will demands that one really be "free"—even free to go astray. And unlike the angels who had but one moment, or crisis, of choice, each individual of mankind has a lifelong series of choices to make. Thus, it stands to reason that at least once, somewhere along the way, each man would choose to go astray—*especially* the first man, Adam, when we consider the interplay of mutinous angelic free will on full display in the Garden. This is just the chaotic nature of true free will that, by definition, concedes that an indestructible Way was unattainable without the direct intervention of God.

But in this very problem associated with the nature of

free will, we see the beauty of—and incredible love and passion within—the plan of God. We see how before the foundation of the world, the triune God planned to directly intervene without limiting in any way the validity and reality of free will. He did this through His incarnation, teaching, miracles, healings, passion, and triumphant descent into Hell, with subsequent resurrection and ascension as the Christ.

The Christ is literally God Incarnate (Emmanuel, God with us), and thus as *the* Man, our Lord made the free will choice at each and every point of decision, at every crisis of choice, to remain in fellowship with the created order of His Father—even under the barrage of mutinous satanic free will on full display at the temptation. Then, after the cross, by the power of His indestructible life, He overcame Satan in the spiritual realm.

The Christ was the only solution to the inherent problem with free will, the only foolproof plan to implement an indestructible Way. The Christ was the only way that God could both create beings with free will *and* provide for the never-ending increase of His Kingdom. There is no other scenario that makes any sense, for no other scenario would allow for rational beings endowed with true free will, while ensuring an unassailable Way into Heaven.

As we come to understand this incredible plan of the triune Living God, and His love for mankind, whereby God the Father would send His Son, and the Son of God

—literally the Word of the Father made flesh—
would sacrifice Himself to make our fellowship with
Him forever possible, we find ourselves saying with the
Apostle Paul, "Frankly, I stand amazed at the depth of
the riches of God's wisdom and knowledge. How
impossible to fully and completely understand are His
judgments; and how inscrutable (see Glossary) His ways!'
For: 'Who has known the mind of the Lord? Or who
has become His counselor?' 'Or who has first given to
Him and it shall be repaid to him?'" (Rom 11:33–35
KJV-ed. PBR) "For everything comes from Him and
exists by His power and is intended for His glory. All
glory to Him forever! Amen!" (Rom 11:36 NLT)

You see, with the veil lifted, it is one of God's great gifts
to mankind that we can come to understand, with the
Apostle Paul, something of the depth of the riches of
God's wisdom and knowledge. The Apostle Paul
confirmed as much so many years ago: "For I am a
minister of the Church by divine commission, a
commission granted to me for your benefit and for a
special purpose: that I might fully declare God's word—
that sacred mystery which up to now has been hidden in
every age and every generation, but which is now as clear
as daylight to those who love God." (Col 1:25–26
Phillips)

This sacred mystery, which is now crystal clear (as clear as
daylight to those who love God), includes free-will beings
who now have access to the indestructible Way—yet no
means by which to destroy this Way. All God ever wanted
was to fellowship for all eternity with His creation—

but only with those who, of their own free will, wanted this fellowship. And that is what God now has ("Jesus answered, and said unto him, 'If any man love me, he will keep my word, and my Father will love him, and we will come unto him, and make our home with him.'" [Jn 14:23 GNV-ed. PBR]).

Now, what do we understand that this fully implemented indestructible Way means to man since the Ascension? Well, even today, some two thousand years after the Ascension, man continues in his two-tier structure so gloriously designed by our loving Creator.

He is born into the material world through the normal means of men, procreation. Then, for those who willingly choose to fellowship with God for all eternity, such men are born again—*literally born a second time!*—this time by the Holy Spirit into the spiritual world. And this birth that translates us into a dimension of a completely different nature from the material world is carried out through the means of faith—choosing to believe—in Jesus Christ.

Those making such a choice during their time on earth, the first tier of mankind's existence, then find that the truth of the teaching of Jesus Christ becomes true for them personally: "And when Jesus was demanded of the Pharisees, when the Kingdom of God should come, He answered them, and said, 'The Kingdom of God cometh not with observation. Neither shall men say, "Lo here," or "lo there:" for behold, the Kingdom of God is within you.'" (Luke 17:20–21 GNV-ed. PBR)

So those who choose to believe in the Son of God, Jesus Christ, will go, at the end of their days here on this earth, into eternal fellowship with God in the metaphysical world of Paradise, this different dimension, this higher plane, which was from the beginning and remains today, the second stage, or second tier, of mankind's eternal existence. This was the plan before time, the plan of the triune God before the foundation of the world. And this eternal Way is now indestructible as the mutinous interplay of free will has been resolved so that the Way can never again be destroyed.

So we find that today mankind continues to provide generation after generation of progeny on this earth, and from each generation, those destined for eternal life by their faith in Jesus Christ become Christians, and obtain for themselves life beyond the bounds of time. We also find that still today the joy of God is secured, as the earth has already, and forever, been reclaimed through its reconciliation (" ... God was in Christ, personally reconciling the world to Himself ...." [2 Cor 5:19 Phillips-ed. PBR]). The Kingdom of Heaven continues to welcome new Christians from each generation, and this increase is without end!

This is why we read that the "glory" of the Nations, that is, those that are born again from all the Nations of this material world, are brought into the Kingdom of God, while non-believers are not able to enter. Note that in the following scene, there remains in the earthly material dimension the Nations, and within those earthly Nations, both the righteous *and* the unclean (those that work abomination and lies):

"And I saw no Temple therein: for the Lord God Almighty and the Lamb are the Temple of it. And this city hath no need of the sun, neither of the moon to shine in it: for the glory of God did light it: and the Lamb is the light of it. And the people which are saved, shall walk in the light of it: and the Kings of the earth shall bring their glory and honor unto it. And the gates of it shall not be shut by day: for there shall be no night there. And the glory, and honor of the Nations shall be brought unto it. And there shall enter into it none unclean thing, neither whatsoever worketh abomination or lies: but they which are written in the Lamb's book of life." (Rv 21:22–27 GNV-ed. PBR)

So the Christ, this historical Jesus who is both fully God and fully man, has already successfully led the way for all men into Paradise. He has already resolved the mutinous conflict inherent in the free will of His creation. This is why we read in Scripture of the Christ and His current and continuing rule as a true partaker of mankind:

"For though in past ages God did grant authority to angels, yet He did not put the future world of men under their control, and it is this world that we are now talking about. But someone has said: 'What is man that You are mindful of him, or the Son of Man that You take care of Him? You made Him a little lower than the angels; You crowned Him with glory and honor, and set Him over the works of Your hands. You have put all things in subjection under His feet ...."' (Heb 2:5–8 Phillips)

So man was made a little lower than the angels (tier one), so that he could obtain a doorway into Paradise (tier two) through *the* Man that was immutable and eternal, and through *this* Man, be forever elevated to his ultimate created position in heaven, which is, in fact, and according to the created order, higher than that of the angels. "He has now entered Heaven and is in the place of supreme honor of God, in Heaven at God's right hand, with all angels, authorities and powers subservient to Him." (1 Pet 3:22 Phillips-ed. PBR)

And what does the Bible say in respect to this wonderful and glorious situation? The Apostle Paul had the following to say:

"Praise be to the God and the Father of our Lord Jesus Christ, for giving us through Christ every possible spiritual benefit as citizens of Heaven! For consider what He has done—before the foundation of the world He chose us to become, in Christ, His holy and blameless children living within His constant care. He planned, in His purpose of love, to adopt us as His own children through Jesus Christ—that we might learn to praise that glorious generosity of His which has made us welcome in the everlasting love He bears towards the Son. It is through the Son, at the cost of His own blood, that we are redeemed, freely forgiven through that full and generous grace which has overflowed into our lives and opened our eyes to the truth. For God has allowed us to know the secret of His plan, and it is this: He purposes in

His sovereign will that all human history shall be consummated in Christ, that everything that exists in Heaven or earth shall find its perfection and fulfillment in Him." (Eph 1:3–10 Phillips-ed. PBR)

Now ask yourself; Can there be any greater plan than this? Any greater love? Can there be any design more incredible than the Increate of the Universe, the creator and sustainer of all things, planning through His triune nature His own suffering, even before time began so that He could bring to mankind (beings He intentionally created with free will) immutable and indestructible access to His unending love in Paradise and a full and complete resolution to the conflict of mutinous free will between the two realms? And this, for all eternity with no chance of ever being disrupted again!

Now Philippians tells us well the incredible nature of the Incarnation that led to these wonderful things:

"Let Christ Himself be your example as to what your attitude should be. For He, Who had always been God by nature, did not cling to His prerogatives as God's equal, but stripped Himself of all privilege, by consenting to be a slave by nature and be born as mortal man. And, having become man, He humbled Himself by living a life of utter obedience, even unto the extent of the death of the body, even the death of His own body as a common criminal on the cross. That is why God has now lifted Him so high, and has given Him the Name above all names, so that at the name of Jesus 'every knee shall bow,' whether in Heaven, or earth, or under the earth.

And that is why, in the end, 'every tongue shall confess' that Jesus Christ is the Lord, to the glory of God the Father." (Phil 2:5–11 Phillips-ed. PBR)

Given this current state of affairs, it behooves us all to take a moment and prayerfully consider *our* choices. You see, being endowed with free will means we are personally responsible for our choices, which means each of us personally faces his own crisis of choice, and this is true of each of us individually in every generation. Will each one of us individually choose Heaven—or Hell and the Lake of Fire?

With this in mind, let us now carefully consider the words of the Apostle Paul:

"As co-operators with God himself, we beg you then, not to fail to use the grace of God. For God's word is—'In an acceptable time I have heard you, and in the day of salvation I have helped you.' Now is the 'acceptable time,' and this very day is the 'day of salvation.'" (2 Cor 6:1–2 Phillips-ed. PBR)

"This means that our knowledge of men can no longer be based on their outward lives (indeed, even though we knew Christ as a man, we do not know Him like that any longer). For if a man is in Christ he becomes a new person altogether—the past is finished and gone, he has become a fresh and new creation. All this is God's doing, for He has reconciled us to Himself through the Christ; and He has made us agents of the reconciliation. God was in Christ personally reconciling the world to Himself—

not counting their sins against them—and has commissioned us with the message of reconciliation. We are now Christ's ambassadors, as though God were appealing direct to you through us. As His personal representatives we say, 'Make your peace with God.' For God caused Christ, who Himself knew nothing of sin, actually to be the offering for our sin, so that in Christ we might be made good with the goodness of God." (2 Cor 5:16–21 Phillips-ed. PBR)

So we need to "make our peace with Jesus Christ," for it is certain that in the end of every life, in the twinkling of an eye, at the moment of translation from this life (tier one) to the next (tier two), whether a believer or not, every soul meets its maker. And in that grand and glorious meeting before the magnificent throne of God, every soul, believer or not, can do nothing but " ... confess, that Jesus Christ is the Lord, to the glory of God the Father." (Phil 2:11 KJV-ed. PBR) Amen! Some will do so unto everlasting life, and some to everlasting banishment from the fellowship of the living God.

So, "just as surely as it is appointed for all men once and only once to die from this material world and after that pass to their judgment" (Heb 9:27 Phillips-ed. PBR), we should just as certainly constantly be on guard, always watching out for the life of our own soul, for in truth we " ... know neither the day nor the hour ... " (Mt 25:13 KJV) of the end of our own lives.

We do not want to find ourselves at the end of our earthly lives, at the moment of translation from this life to the next, speechless and hearing directly from the Lord Jesus such terrible words as these: " ... 'Friend, how camest thou in hither, and hast not on a wedding garment?' And he was speechless. Then said the King to the servants, 'Bind him hand and foot: take him away, and cast him into utter darkness: there shall be weeping and gnashing of teeth.'" (Mt 22:12–13 GNV-ed. PBR)

And so today, with the indestructible Way in place, the enemies of Christ have but limited options. In truth, their only ploy left should now be plain to us, for to be successful, they must so destroy the nations of this world such that no one "can" believe. They must so destroy Christianity such that this generation, and the next one after that, and so on and so forth, no longer send any saints to heaven. They must make it so that there is no "glory" of the nations.

You see, this is the specific goal of the enemies of Christ. They seek to ensure that there are no more true Christians. This is the motive of the enemies of Christ as they have sought to dismantle every Christian nation since the cross. This is the motive of the enemies of Christ as they currently seek to dismantle the once great Western Christian World. This will be the motive of the enemies of Christ as they will seek in the future to dismantle every great Christian nation that comes after us. It is the only card in their hand left to play.

Therefore, Christians—we must be on *guard*, be *counted*, and make our voices *heard*. We must ensure that we can not only stop the enemies of Christ, but also overcome them and increase the numbers of saints going to heaven from our generation.

This is one of man's most basic fundamental duties during his life. It is connected to his most fundamental duty under the law of the living God, starting with the commandment to love our Lord and our God—Jesus Christ, the only name by which we can be saved, and ending with the commandment to love your neighbor as yourself. Following these two laws will ensure the greatest numbers of saints, from each generation, will enter the City of God.

Day One of Creation

Chapter One

With the understanding that Jesus Christ is God Incarnate—Emmanuel, God with us, the visible expression of the invisible God, the Increate of the universe by whom the world began; by whom mankind received the indestructible Way; by whom mankind was freed from the horror of captivity under the prince of darkness; by whom the mutinous interplay of free will within the creation has been resolved; and by whom the never-ending growth of the Kingdom of God is generated; we find the starting point from which we can rationally, and in the context of eternal Christendom, study the Christian beginnings as they are found in Genesis Chapter One.

As we begin our study, recall that we cannot help but read Scripture with the veil off, as Christ has lifted the veil for all of us in Christendom. In fact, it is indeed offensive to us to study Genesis without Jesus Christ being recognized as the visible manifestation of that triune God who created the heaven and the earth, for "In the beginning Jesus Christ created the heaven and the earth." (Gn 1:1 LXX-ed. PBR) This is the beginning of the Bible and the premise for our study.

As we examine this verse within the context of eternal Christendom, notice that God did not create multiple heavens or multiple earths, but just one heaven and one earth. The heaven. The earth. The metaphysical realm. The physical realm. The spiritual world. The material world. The heavenly dimension. The earthly dimension.

From this, we can conclude that there are not multiple universes or multiple planets in or upon which life exists. There is but this one heaven and this one earth, and the whole of the material creation surrounding this one earth exists to support life on this one planet. There is no life in this material universe apart from the life on this earth. There are, as one might say, no "extraterrestrials."

We also see from this verse that the creation was a *fiat* creation. Fiat means "a command or act of will that creates something without … further effort" (see Glossary). In other words, something was made from nothing (*ex nihilo*—from or out of nothing, see Glossary), by just the command of God.

Prior to Genesis 1:1, there was only the triune God, the unique Increate of all that was, is, or ever will be. Then, by nothing more than the command of this Increate God, the heaven and the earth simply came into existence. There was no "Big Bang;" God the Father simply created the heaven and the earth by His command (by His Word, Jesus Christ—"In the beginning was the Word, and the Word was with God, and the Word was God." [Jn 1:1 KJV]). He spoke, and it then existed (creation by *fiat, ex nihilo!*).

So the creation came into being simply from the decree of God the Father by the work of Jesus Christ. Nothing more than His Word (Jesus Christ) brought into being the whole of heaven and earth.

And God fully sustains the whole creation, for nothing created can sustain itself, and because everything but God is created, everything is sustained by Jesus Christ, who is the "word of His power." (see Heb 1:3) The heaven and the earth were created by God and will continue on forever and ever as each is powered and sustained by the eternal self-existing uncreated triune God Himself ("And He built His sanctuary like high palaces, like the earth which He hath established forever." [Ps 78:69 KJV-ed. PBR] "Who establishes the earth on her sure foundation: it shall not be moved forever." [Ps 104:5 LXX-ed. PBR]).

Looking further at the status of the earthly dimension immediately following creation, we find: "But the earth was invisible and unformed, and darkness was over the deep, and the Spirit of God moved upon the water." (Gn 1:2 LXX-ed. PBR)

What we learn from this is that the earth, at its creation, was completely covered in water; there was no land appearing anywhere on its surface. The land was invisible, and darkness was over the deep. There was no trace of light anywhere in the creation, as of yet. In essence, the earth was a large body of water without form. It was void, empty, without life, covered in total darkness, sitting by itself, held in place only " ... by the Word of His power

…." (Heb 1:3 KJV-ed. PBR)

Then the One and Only Spirit of God "moved upon" this created body of water, which was the earth. Consider the words of Job as he spoke of this great Creator God: "Who alone has stretched out the heavens, and walks on the sea as on firm ground." (Jb 9:8 LXX) Job is referring to this time spoken of in Genesis 1:2 when God walked upon the waters of the earth as if on firm ground. Even more amazing, consider the words of Mark, which also identify this same God walking on the water as if upon firm ground: "And He *(Jesus)* saw them troubled in rowing, (for the wind was contrary unto them), and about the fourth watch of the night, He came unto them, walking upon the sea …." (Mark 6:48 GNV-ed. PBR)

Thus, with the veil lifted, we can understand that Jesus Christ is that visible expression of the very same One who in Genesis 1:2 moved upon or "walked upon" the water!

Having elaborated a bit on the state of the material creation as of day one, let us now examine how God proceeded with the day one creation and formation of the spiritual Kingdom within the newly created metaphysical Heaven. "And God said, 'Let there be light,' and there was light." (Gn 1:3–4 LXX-ed. PBR)

This light created here on day one, this light of God the Father, created by His Word Jesus Christ, was not the sun, the moon, nor the stars, for these were all created on day four in the material dimension. No, this light created on day one was nothing less than all of the metaphysical spiritual Kingdom of God, which includes the throne of God, the "New Jerusalem" or "City of God," all the different and unique angels created in their fully mature form, Hell, Tartarus, the bottomless pit, the Lake of Fire, and Paradise.

"And God saw the light that it was good, and God *(Jesus Christ)* divided between the light and the darkness." (Gn 1:3–4 LXX-ed. PBR) The division between the light and the darkness here spoken of was an eternal division between the metaphysical world, or the heaven created in verse one, and the physical material world, or the earth created in that selfsame verse. The darkness here spoken of in this decree separating the two worlds is not "evil," or the devil, or any such thing, as even on day seven, the Lord tells us that everything was "good"—meaning that not even Satan had fallen yet. No, this darkness is simply the darkness over the deep, the darkness still present in the material world and elaborated upon in verse two as previously noted. Remember, the sun, moon, and stars had not yet been created in the material world; only the heaven and the earth had been created, and the earth was invisible and unformed and darkness was over the deep.

So this Kingdom of Light, created by our Lord and our God Jesus Christ (see John 20:28), was of a different type or different kind than anything that would ever be created in the material world. It was of a completely different dimension than that of the material world. In this dimension of the Kingdom of Light—totally separate and distinct from the material world—there was not, is not now, and never will be any sun, moon, or stars; there is but the glory of the triune God, and it is this glory that provides the light of this metaphysical world.

Hear the words of our Lord to this effect as shared with us in the book of The Revelation to John: "And I saw no Temple therein: for the Lord God Almighty and the Lamb are the Temple of it. And this city hath no need of the sun, neither of the moon to shine in it: for the glory of God did light it; and the Lamb is the light of it." (Rv 21:22–23 GNV-ed. PBR) "And there shall be no night there, and they need no candle, neither light of the sun: for the Lord God giveth them light, and they shall reign for evermore." (Rv 22:5 GNV-ed. PBR)

So even after mankind had sinned and lost their Way to the tree of life, the tree of life remained in the city of this Kingdom of Light: "In the midst of the street of it, and of either side of the river, was there the tree of life: which bare twelve manner of fruits: and gave fruit every month: and the leaves of the tree served to heal the people." (Rv 22:2 Tyndale-ed. PBR)

This glorious Kingdom of Light, created by Jesus Christ on day one of the creation, and which includes the literal formation of everything that is within the created heaven referred to in the verse "In the beginning God created the heaven and the earth" (Gn 1:1 LXX-ed. PBR), *is* the tier two into which mankind was meant to enter, and remains so yet today. Mankind was always intended to be born into this material world, and after each individual's time on this earth (tier one) was complete, he was to enter the Kingdom of Light (tier two). Hear the word of our Lord as recorded for us in Colossians:

"You will even be able to thank God in the midst of pain and distress because you are privileged to share the lot of those who are living in the light. For we must never forget that He rescued us from the power of darkness, and transferred us into the Kingdom of His beloved Son, that is, into the Kingdom of Light." (Col 1:12–13 Phillips-ed. PBR)

Men of faith living in this first tier of existence have, throughout recorded history, always looked for their eternal life, and second tier of existence, in the spiritual realm, for they have all " … freely admitted that they lived on this earth as strangers and pilgrims. Men who say that mean, of course, that their eyes are fixed upon their true homeland. If they had meant the particular country they had left behind, they had ample opportunity to return. No, the fact is that they longed for a better country altogether, nothing less than a heavenly one. And because of this faith of theirs, God is not ashamed to be called their God for in sober truth He has prepared for them a city in Heaven." (Heb 11:13–16 Phillips-ed. PBR)

As an example of the spiritual realm being our true second tier of existence, we have Enoch, Moses, and Elijah. Each of these entered this Kingdom of Light after his time in this material world was complete, even before the Way had been re-opened for mankind as a whole. Hear the word of our Lord as found in the book of Hebrews in regard to Enoch:

"It was because of his faith that Enoch was translated to the eternal world without experiencing death. He disappeared from this world because God transferred him from this world to heaven, and before that happened his reputation was that 'he pleased God.'" (Heb 11:5 Phillips-ed. PBR)

Hear the word of our Lord as found in the book of Jude with regard to Moses: "Whereas Michael, the archangel, when contending with the devil in the dispute concerning the 'body' of Moses, dared not bring a judgment of blasphemy, but rather said, 'The Lord rebuke you.'" (Jude 1:9 KJV-ed. PBR)

The contention referred to here occurred because Moses, who actually did physically die, nevertheless had his spirit taken by Michael, the archangel, straight to heaven, skipping Hell. Satan wanted and contended for the spirit body of Moses to put it in Hell with the rest of his captives. But the Lord took Moses, as He had taken Enoch before him (though slightly differently, as Enoch did not actually physically die), directly from this earth into Heaven.

Now, hear the word of our Lord as found in the book of Second Kings with regard to Elijah: "And it came to pass as they *(Elijah and Elisha)* were going, they went on talking; and, behold, a chariot of fire, and horses of fire, and it separated between them both; and Elijah was taken up in a whirlwind as it were into heaven." (2 Kings

2:11 LXX-ed. PBR) Elijah was essentially "translated" into the Kingdom of Light (tier two) directly from this material world (tier one).

Please also note with regard to these three men and their early arrival in Heaven—which was but a foreshadowing of the ultimate Ascension of Christ—that at the transfiguration of the Christ, we see two of them talking with Jesus. How could this have been?

Well, from the verses above we learned that they were all taken directly to Heaven, never going down to Hell or held captive by Satan in his evil domain. Thus, they were all, even within the boundaries of time during the earthly life and earthly ministry of Jesus Christ, in Heaven. Therefore, they were available, and two of them, Moses and Elijah, actually appeared with Jesus at His transfiguration, appearing out of Heaven, wherein they dwelt even before the actualization in time of the resurrection and ascension.

Now, one final note regarding this creation of light: The Kingdom of Light Jesus Christ creates on day one, is also referred to in Scripture as "the third heaven." Hear the words of our Lord as recorded for us in Second Corinthians when Paul was describing his being taken up into this heavenly Kingdom: "I know a man in Christ who, fourteen years ago … had the experience of being caught up into the third Heaven." (2 Cor 12:2 Phillips)

Now remember, we read the Bible with the veil lifted. Therefore, we can understand that the creation of the

Kingdom of Light on day one is this selfsame third Heaven into which the Apostle Paul was here caught up. On day two we will see what the first and second heaven are, and then we will understand why this spiritual heaven is referred to in Scripture as the "third" heaven.

Continuing on, recall that previously on day one, "God *(Jesus Christ)* divided between the light and the darkness." And we saw that with these words the Lord put an eternal division between the spiritual world and the material world. When we now, then, proceed to read, "And God called the light Day, and the darkness He called Night, and there was evening and there was morning, the first day" (Gn 1:5 LXX-ed. PBR), we need to understand what these words are telling us. The division between the metaphysical and physical worlds was already complete, so we can understand that these words must have another meaning. In fact, what we find is that they do not have just "another" meaning but instead they are prophetically naming two yet future things.

The first thing we learn from God here calling the light Day, and the darkness Night, is that day and night in the material world will forever take their name from this very verse. We all know that during the time the sun is up in the sky, we call it "day," and when there is darkness, and the moon and stars are up, we call it "night." But remember when God first said these words, there was yet no sun, no moon, and no stars, so the statement was prophetic, and stating what would soon come to pass.

There is a second thing we learn from God here calling

the light Day, and the darkness Night, and it is related to the endowing of created beings with free will; for our Lord knew that chaos must of necessity ensue from such a created order. He knew that by necessity, some of the already created angels must fall. He knew that by necessity the soon-to-be-created mankind must fall. So the Lord is here showing us prophetically the nature of His creation as it must be—otherwise there would not have actually been true free will!

To see this other, deeper, nature of this calling of the light Day, and the darkness Night, hear the words of our Lord in First Thessalonians: "You are all sons of light, sons of the day, and none of us belongs to darkness or the night." (1 Thes 5:5 Phillips) And in First Peter: "But you are God's 'chosen race,' His 'royal priesthood,' His 'holy nation,' His 'peculiar people'—all the old titles of God's people now belong to you. It is for you now to demonstrate the goodness of Him who has called you out of darkness into His marvelous light. In the past you were not 'a people' at all: but now you are the people of God! In the past you had no experience of His mercy, but now it is intimately yours!" (1 Pet 2:9–10 Phillips-ed. PBR)

Yes, this second prophetic meaning of this calling of the light Day, and the darkness Night, was in reference to the darkness of sin that would ultimately come, and the glory of the light that would ultimately drown out that darkness.

So " ... there was evening and there was morning, the

first day." (Gn 1:5 LXX) In this simple statement our
Lord lets us know that we have now completed our first
twenty-four hour period. The Lord was already keeping
time; thus, He says there was evening and there was
morning. Yet still there was total darkness throughout the
material portion of the creation; while there was perfect
light in the spiritual creation.

Day Two of Creation

Chapter Two

And God said, 'Let there be a firmament in the midst of the water, and let it separate upwards in the midst of the water and water,' and it was so. And God (*Jesus Christ*) made the firmament, and God (*Jesus Christ*) separated it upwards in the midst of the water which was under the firmament and separated it upwards in the midst of the water which was above the firmament. And God called the firmament Heaven, and God saw that it was good, and there was evening and there was morning, the second day." (Gn 1:6–8 LXX-ed. PBR)

In studying these verses that describe the creation activities of the second day, the first thing to make note of is that the term "Heaven" now takes on an additional meaning. The first meaning was the whole of the spiritual realm created on day one, and specifically referred to in Scripture as the third heaven. The second meaning now assigned to the word is this material firmament that is here, on day two, created to encircle the earth.

In order to understand this Heaven of day two, we need to realize from these words that Jesus Christ, the very Word of God the Father, is creating a material expanse stretching out from the very earth itself, stretching it from the earth upward and outward. An expanse, further, that is in two parts.

The first part is the atmosphere that expands upwards from the water on the earth to the just then created water canopy, which from that time forward until the flood, surrounded the earth. The second part is the rest of space, or "outer space," that expands upward from the water that was just then placed above the earth all the way to the ends of the material creation.

These two firmaments, referred to by induction as the first heaven and the second heaven, now provide the expanse of the material universe created by Jesus Christ. From this understanding, we can see why Job said of God during His creative acts: "Who alone has *stretched out* the heavens ...." (Jb 9:8 LXX, italics mine)

Remembering the heaven of day one (the third heaven, that spiritual metaphysical heaven in which the Kingdom of Light resides), understand now that this third heaven is that through which this "stretched out from the earth itself " material expanse was extended. While the two are of a completely different nature or dimension, eternally separated by the Word of God, they yet exist without confusion within one another.

Recall back to day one when Jesus Christ created "the heaven and the earth," and understand now that even from day one, the metaphysical heaven completely surrounded the earth, even though it was of a completely different dimension. Now on day two, we see the physical dimension being filled with the material expanse to correlate with the existence of this third heaven—even while the two remain totally separate and distinct.

"And God called the firmament Heaven, and God saw that it was good …." (Gn 1:8 LXX-ed. PBR) In this portion of the verse, this Heaven being referred to is the just created material expanse or firmament, the whole of the material Heaven, both the earth's atmosphere and all the rest of space beyond the earth's atmosphere (outer space). That is, all of heaven one and two but not including the third heaven or the spiritual world.

So we see then that on day two the earth is still all covered by water, and there is yet no dry land to be seen. But the earth is now firmly set within the firmament. The firmament encircles it, having been stretched upward and outward from the very surface water of the earth, in preparation for the continuing development toward life on earth.

" … And there was evening and there was morning, the second day." (Gn 1:8 LXX) The Lord finishes the account of day two by letting us know that we have now completed our second twenty-four hour day. God was indeed keeping time. And as was true on the first day, on this second day there was still total darkness throughout the material universe. There was yet no sun or moon or stars and therefore no light in the physical dimension of the creation.

Day Three of Creation

Chapter Three

And God said, 'Let the water which is under the heaven be collected into one place, and let the dry land appear,' and it was so. And the water which was under the heaven was collected into its places, and the dry land appeared." (Gn 1:9 LXX-ed. PBR)

In these verses, the heaven referred to is the first heaven, or the firmament which is the "atmosphere" of the earth. The water referred to is the water on the earth, which is under the first heaven. Then we see that as this water on the earth and under the first heaven is collected into its places, the dry land appears for the first time.

"And God called the dry land Earth, and the gatherings of waters He called Seas, and God saw that it was good." (Gn 1:10 LXX-ed. PBR) So as was true of the term "heaven," the term "earth" now takes on a second meaning, the first meaning being the whole globe, the second meaning now being made clear to us is the visible dry land of this globe. This original dry land that became visible was most likely one super continent that more than likely spread all across the globe.

The gatherings of the waters referred to in these verses is plural. We understand from this that there were bodies of waters on this dry land such as rivers, as we see in Genesis, chapter two, when the original Garden of Eden is described:

"And a river proceeds out of Eden to water the Garden, thence it divides itself into four heads. The name of the one, Phisom, this it is which encircles the whole land of Evilat, where there is gold. And the gold of that land is good, there also is carbuncle and emerald. And the name of the second river is Geon, this it is which encircles the whole land of Ethiopia. And the third river is Tigris, this is that which flows forth over against the Assyrians. And the fourth river is Euphrates." (Gn 2:10–14 LXX-ed. PBR)

Something to make note of regarding this description is that it does not provide the location of the Garden on the earth as we know it today. The truth is that this land of Eden described here by our Lord was destroyed in the worldwide flood of Noah's day. Also, as the gatherings of the waters referred to in these verses is plural, it speaks to there also being various lakes to go along with the Sea or Seas formed across this one land mass. And God saw that it was good, and then proceeded with His creation.

"And God said, 'Let the earth bring forth the herb of grass bearing seed according to its kind and according to its likeness, and the fruit-tree bearing fruit whose seed is in it, according to its kind on the earth,' and it was so. And the earth brought forth the herb of grass bearing seed according to its kind and according to its likeness, and the fruit tree bearing fruit whose seed is in it, according to its kind on the earth, and God saw that it was good." (Gn 1:11–12 LXX-ed. PBR) From these verses we see that not only did the dry land appear on day three, but the vegetation of the earth was created as well.

But this creation of the vegetation was just a bit different from what we have seen thus far. For in this day three creation of the vegetation, we do not have a creation such that this vegetation is now formed and growing on the earth and in the sea. Remember, we have the earth still in total darkness as there is yet no sun, moon, or stars in the sky, so these plants could not have lived even for a day. This understanding is confirmed for us in Genesis chapter two where we learn:

"This is the book of the generation of heaven and earth, when they were made, in the day in which the Lord God *(Jesus Christ)* made the heaven and the earth, and every herb of the field *before* it was on the earth, and all the grass of the field *before* it sprang up, for God had not rained on the earth, and there was not a man to cultivate it." (Gn 2:4–5 LXX-ed. PBR, italics mine)

So we see that while here on day three Jesus Christ does indeed create the vegetation of the earth, nevertheless He does not cause it to actually yet spring forth upon the earth.

We will see later in Genesis that our Lord, after the first full week of creation, does bring forth a watering of the dry land: "But there rose a fountain out of the earth, and watered the whole face of the earth." (Gn 2:6 LXX)

Therefore, we understand that only after this watering of

the dry land will the vegetation of the dry land then be growing. Here, on day three, we have but the creation of the vegetation of the earth and sea, no bringing forth yet its actual growth.

We also have on day three our first mention of the law of kind after kind, codified in the Ten Commandments as "Thou shalt not adulterate." And this law was meant to be specifically followed by all the material creation living on the earth, thus its mention in conjunction with the very beginning or creation of actual life on the earth. This law of kind after kind is one of great importance, for "blaspheming the heavenly order" is literally the breaking of this most important commandment.

"And there was evening and there was morning, the third day." (Gn 1:13 LXX) From this verse we know that we have now completed our third twenty-four hour day. And as was true on the first and second days, the Lord was already keeping time even though there was still total darkness throughout the material universe. There was not yet sun, nor moon, nor stars, and therefore no light in the physical dimension of the creation.

Day Four of Creation

Chapter Four

And God said, 'Let there be lights in the firmament of the heaven to give light upon the earth, to divide between day and night' ...." (Gn 1:14 LXX-ed. PBR) In this verse, the firmament of the heaven into which these lights are placed is the second heaven, or outer space, where we see these lights yet today.

Further, to confirm that the evening and the morning from the first three twenty-four hour days all occurred in the darkness, the Lord here tells us that He is putting these lights into the firmament of the heaven "to divide between day and night." This confirms our understanding that during the previous three days the Lord had been keeping time, and there actually had been day and night, but no division by light and darkness.

This also confirms our understanding that the initial division between light and darkness that occurred on day one was not between "day and night" of the physical material world, but instead a division between the third heaven, or the spiritual metaphysical dimension, and the material or earthly dimension.

" ... 'And let them be for signs and for seasons and for days and for years. And let them be for light in the firmament of the heaven, so as to shine upon the earth,' and it was so. And God *(Jesus Christ)* made the two great lights, the greater light for regulating the day and the lesser light for regulating the night, the stars also. And God *(Jesus Christ)* placed them in the firmament of the heaven, so as to shine upon the earth, and to regulate day and night, and to divide between the light and the darkness. And God saw that it was good." (Gn 1:14–18 LXX-ed. PBR)

In these verses, we should understand that again the firmament of the heaven being referred to is the second heaven, outer space, as this is where the sun, moon and stars were placed—and where we find them yet today. This firmament is in the heaven expanding upward from the end of the earth's atmosphere to the edge and end of the material universe.

From these verses we can conclude that the earth truly is the center of all activity throughout the material "heaven" or material universe. It is the focal point of the whole material creation. The earth was created to provide the birthing center for the children of promise, the heirs of salvation from among the sons of Adam, each of whose true home, as spiritual beings, would ultimately be in the third heaven. This is why all the lights in the heaven are for signs and for seasons and for days and for years to none but the inhabitants of this one earth.

Another thing to make note of here is a continuation of something we learned from day three. Recall that on day three Jesus Christ created all the vegetation of the earth, but it was not yet brought forth. The vegetation did not grow either on the dry land nor in the sea because there was yet no sun, moon or stars in the sky. But here now on day four, we *do* have the sun, moon and stars in the sky, so we have to ask ourselves, "What effect would this have on the created but not yet formed vegetation throughout both the dry land and the land under the sea?"

The answer is that on the dry land, the sun, moon and stars would have no immediate effect on the created but not yet formed vegetation for there was still no watering of the dry land upon the earth. So the vegetation would remain created but not yet in bloom across all of the dry land.

But in the sea, which is of course water upon "dry land," or put another way, earth under water, the answer is that the sun, moon, and stars had a very powerful effect. In essence, upon the creation here on day four of the sun, moon, and stars, all the vegetation in the sea sprang forth in their fully mature forms. This provided in the seas a perfect environment for the bringing forth of the living moving creatures that lived in the water. And we will see this natural progression proceeding forward on day five in the very next chapter.

"And there was evening and there was morning, the fourth day." (Gn 1:19 LXX) In this verse, the Lord lets us know that we have now completed our fourth twenty-four hour day. But, unlike days one, two or three, there is now actual darkness and light in this material physical world to go along with the keeping of time through the evening and the morning on this, the fourth day. And still today we have this darkness and light from the sun and moon and stars to go along with the keeping of time, the evening and the morning, of each of our days.

Day Five of Creation

Chapter Five

And God said, 'Let the waters bring forth living moving creatures having life, and winged flying creatures flying above the earth in the firmament of heaven,' and it was so." (Gn 1:20 LXX-ed. PBR) In this verse, the reference to the firmament of heaven "above the earth" is the first heaven, the atmosphere of our earth. This is of course where we yet today find the winged flying creatures—flying above the earth in the first heaven.

"And God *(Jesus Christ)* made great huge sea creatures, and every living moving creature, which the waters brought forth according to their kinds, and every winged flying creature according to its kind, and God saw that they were good. And God blessed them saying, 'Increase and multiply and fill the waters in the seas, and let the flying creatures be multiplied on the earth.'" (Gn 1:21–22 LXX-ed. PBR)

Before discussing these verses further, recall that on day three we learned that Jesus Christ created all the vegetation, but the vegetation did not spring forth on that day. In fact we saw that not until after day seven does the vegetation on the dry land spring forth. And on day four we saw that the vegetation in the seas sprang forth upon the creation of the sun, moon and stars.

With this reminder, we can now understand that,

following this same pattern, we have here on day five the actual creation *and* formation of the living moving creatures of the sea. This was possible because the vegetation in its fully mature form had already sprung forth in the seas on day four.

However, we have only the creation of the winged flying creatures according to their kind on this day, not their actual formation. A quick review should help you understand why, for certainly the winged flying creatures would have water that they could drink from the existent seas and rivers, but they had no vegetation upon the dry land which they would need in order to survive. Thus the Lord Jesus Christ here creates, but does not yet form these winged flying creatures until after day seven of the creation.

See later in Genesis where their actual formation occurs: "And God *(Jesus Christ)* formed yet still out of the earth all the wild beasts of the field, and all the flying creatures of the sky, and He brought them to Adam, to see what he would call them, and whatever Adam called any living creature, that was the name of it." (Gn 2:19 LXX-ed. PBR)

We can therefore conclude that all of this from day five makes perfect sense, and is in keeping with the continuing progression of the first week of creation. We now have the seas filled with every living moving creature which God created to live in the water, and we have the winged flying creatures—the birds, created, but not yet formed.

"And there was evening and there was morning, the fifth day." (Gn 1:23 LXX) Here in this verse the Lord lets us know that we have now completed our fifth twenty-four hour day. And like day four, and every day thereafter, there is actual darkness and light in this material physical world to go along with the keeping of time, the evening and the morning.

Day Six of Creation

Chapter Six

And God said, 'Let the earth bring forth the living creature according to its kind, quadrupeds and creeping things and wild beasts of the earth according to their kind,' and it was so. And God *(Jesus Christ)* made the wild beasts of the earth according to their kind, and cattle according to their kind, and all the creeping things of the earth according to their kind, and God saw that they were good." (Gn 1:24–25 LXX-ed. PBR)

Before discussing these verses, again recall that on day three we learned that Jesus Christ created all the vegetation, but the vegetation did not spring forth on that day. In fact we saw that not until after day seven does the vegetation on the dry land spring forth. With this reminder, we can now understand that, according to this same pattern, here on day six we have only the creation of the living creatures that move on the earth, according to their kind, but not their actual formation.

Again, a quick review should help you understand why, for certainly all the living creatures that move on the earth would have water that they could drink from the existent seas and rivers, but there was no vegetation upon the dry land which they would need in order to survive. Thus the Lord here creates but does not yet form these living creatures that move on the earth—until after day seven.

See for yourself in Genesis where their actual formation occurs: "And God *(Jesus Christ)* formed yet farther out of the earth all the wild beasts of the field, and all the birds of the sky, and He brought them to Adam, to see what he would call them, and whatever Adam called any living creature, that was the name of it. And Adam gave names to all the cattle and to all the birds of the sky, and to all the wild beasts of the field, but for Adam there was not found a help like to himself." (Gn 2:19–20 LXX-ed. PBR)

We can therefore conclude that while these living creatures were created on day six before Adam, they were not actually formed until after the initial seven day creation week. Actually, not until after the literal formation of Adam.

Something else to understand regarding these verses is the phrase "the living creature." In this phrase, God covers "all the living creatures that move on the earth," much as He did with the phrase "every living moving creature" that the sea brought forth. In addition, He also calls out general categories for these living creatures of the earth, those that are of greater value to men—or the quadrupeds or "cattle," which include cows, sheep, horses, etc., animals that actually make up the flocks and herds of men which in ancient times constituted great wealth; and those that are "wild" and do not live with man in a "tamed" environment, creatures such as lions and tigers, etc.; and creepy crawly things such as worms and insects such as ants and beetles and other bugs, etc. of the earth —all the "creeping things that creep on the earth."

Continuing, we see further on this day six: "And God said, 'Let us make man according to our image and likeness, and let them have dominion over the fish of the sea, and over the flying creatures of heaven, and over the cattle and all the earth, and over all the creeping things that creep on the earth.'" (Gn 1:26 LXX-ed. PBR)

In this verse, the terms "us" and "our" are used in reference to the fact that God is speaking in the presence of the angels. Recall that the angels were created on day one as a part of the Kingdom of Light, and so certainly are available to be interacting at this point with God, who was literally speaking His creation into existence (we will see shortly the progression to the singular for the actual description of the act of the creation of man by God).

And making man in "our" image, meant He was making man according to the image of free will beings who would also participate in the Kingdom of Light, even though they would begin their existence, each one individually, in the material world. This is therefore where we learn that this mankind would be the third player involved in the interplay of free will within the creation.

"And God *(Jesus Christ)* made man, according to the image of God He made him, male and female He made them." (Gn 1:27 LXX-ed. PBR) In this verse we see the progression to the singular God for the actual act of the creation of man; as opposed to the "us" and "our" involved in the discussion prior to the creation. We see that He, the singular triune God, not us, the angels and

God, made man in His own image—that image of a free will being like that described with the "us" and "our" (which included God and the angels) of the previous verse.

Of course, we have here the same situation as above for the living creatures that move upon the earth—that is we have on day six the creation of man but not yet the formation of man. Jesus Christ did not in fact actually form man at this point. The reason for this should be apparent by now—the earth had not yet brought forth any vegetation, as God had not yet caused it to rain upon the earth, therefore there was not yet anything for man to eat upon the earth. And this proper understanding of the creation of man, without yet the formation of man here on day six, allows the Christian to rebut the false "kabbalah fable" (see Titus 1:14) relating to the mythical Lilith.

We will soon see that Jesus Christ actually formed the first man, Adam, after the first week of creation in Genesis, chapter two, after He, through the watering of the earth, had brought forth the vegetation in its fully mature form across the previously dry land. We will also see that this formation of man was actually before the forming of the cattle and wild beasts of the field and the winged flying creatures of the first heaven.

"And God blessed them, saying, 'Increase and multiply, and fill the earth and subdue it, and have dominion over the fish of the seas and flying creatures of heaven, and all the cattle and all the earth, and all the creeping things that creep upon the earth.'" (Gn 1:28 LXX-ed. PBR)

In this verse we learn some additional very important points, starting with the point that man was to be the highest of God's material creation—far from being a "scar" upon the land as he is often portrayed by the enemies of Christ. Further, we learn that man is designed specifically to have dominion over all the earth —but this verse is even more specific than just "man" as a whole, for with the veil lifted, we come to understand that this verse is meant specifically for those men born again as Christians into eternal Christendom, as confirmed in the book of Revelation:

"And from Jesus Christ, which is that faithful witness, and that firstborn of the dead, and that Ruler of the kings of the earth. To Him who loves us and has freed us from our sins by His blood, and made us a Kingdom, priests unto God, even His Father, to Him I say be glory and dominion forever and ever. Amen." (Rv 1:5–6 GNV-ed. PBR) "And hast made us a Kingdom, and priests unto our God, and we shall reign on the earth." (Rv 5:10 GNV-ed. PBR)

What a training ground for man's ultimate role in heaven! Of course, it is up to each generation of man to determine if that dominion be for the good of all—only possible when done in fellowship with Jesus Christ, the Word of the living God; or if that dominion be for the punishment and enslavement of all—only possible when done blasphemously, and in direct rebellion to Jesus

Christ and His created order.

"And God said, 'Behold, I have given to you every seed-bearing herb sowing seed which is upon all the earth, and every tree which has in itself the fruit of seed that is sown, to you it shall be for food. And to all the wild beasts of the earth, and to all the flying creatures of heaven, and to every creeping thing that creeps upon the earth, which has in itself the breath of life, even every green plant for food;' and it was so." (Gn 1:29–30 LXX-ed. PBR)

In these verses God separates that of the vegetation which was for man's nourishment, and that of the vegetation which was for the nourishment of the other living creatures. To man was given certain of the vegetation for food, and for the others He gave certain of the green plants for food, to go along with whatever else they might eat.

And this last line—and whatever else they might eat—is important, for what we mean by this last part is that the natural world included from the start, animals that were carnivores. We need to realize as a part of our understanding of these verses, that in them, our Lord does not make both man and animal vegetarians. The Lord gives man a vegetarian diet, and then points out that the animals will eat another portion of the vegetation growing on the earth. According to Scripture, man became a meat eater after the flood, by God's decree in Genesis 9:3 ("Every moving thing that liveth shall be meat for you; even as the green herb have I given you all things." [Gn 9:3 KJV]). But Scripture never makes any decree of change regarding the conversion of animal eating habits, and the only sensible conclusion to this is that the animal kingdom from the very beginning already included vegetarians, meat eaters and combinations thereof.

The value of this understanding is simple, death in the material world has nothing whatsoever to do with death in the spiritual sense that Adam came to understand it after his sin. This is something you will come to see more and more as we proceed.

"And God saw all the things that He had made, and, behold, they were very good ...." (Gn 1:31 LXX-ed. PBR)

From this very important verse we can rest assured that none of the creation that was created with free will had yet fallen. Man was created but not yet formed, so he had not yet sinned. And the angels who were both created and formed in the Kingdom of Light on day one, and were in the presence of God when He announced the creation of man on day six, had not yet reached their decision point. Their hour of decision, their crisis of choice, was coming soon.

" ... And there was evening and there was morning, the sixth day." (Gn 1:31 LXX) The Lord lets us know here in this verse that we have now completed our sixth twenty-four hour day. And like day four and five, and every day thereafter, there is actual darkness and light in this material physical world to go along with the keeping of time, the evening and the morning.

Day Seven of Creation

Chapter Seven

"And the heavens and the earth were finished, and the whole world of them. And God finished on the sixth day His works which He made, and He rested on the seventh day from all His works which He made. And God blessed the seventh day and sanctified it, because in it, He rested from all His works which He began to do." (Gn 2:1–3 LXX-ed. PBR)

In these verses we have the initial creation week brought to a close, though we understand from the events of this initial creation week, that the formation of all that was created is not yet complete. Thus we find after learning of His rest in verse three, that He is resting from all His works "which He *began* to do."

This is no throw-away line, for it confirms our reading that Jesus did have more work to do, that in fact He had not already formed all that He had created. Reading with the veil lifted, as we have been doing, we understand that while everything was indeed already created, not everything was yet formed, thus our Lord makes it clear that He is resting, not from works that are "completed" but works that He "began" to do. This line clarifies for the reader that indeed God was not yet finished with His work. Indeed, His work continues even today ("But Jesus answered them, 'My Father worketh hitherto, and I work.'" [Jn 5:17 GNV-ed. PBR]).

We also have in these verses the blessing and sanctifying of the Sabbath.

Regarding this sanctified Sabbath, it is of great import that we come to understand it without the veil as well, for the veil covering our understanding of the Sabbath has also been lifted by Christ.

We must understand that in the past, the Sabbath was on Saturday—we must also understand that the pathway associated with the Saturday Sabbath is a pathway eternally connected with a "destructible," and now already "destroyed," Way. That is, the Way from tier one unto the rest spoken of in tier two was not indestructible on day seven of creation, and was actually destroyed soon after the formation of Adam.

This is a vital point, for this eternal association of the old Saturday Sabbath with an already destroyed pathway from tier one to tier two is somehow yet celebrated today—by those who refuse to let go of the past. They do this to their own detriment, and in their own folly, for clinging to a way long ago triumphantly replaced makes it impossible for them to enter Paradise through that indestructible Way now fully and completely implemented by that indestructible life of Jesus Christ.

To more fully understand the importance of the Sabbath day question, we need to understand that the final Saturday Sabbath of all time was that Saturday that Jesus Christ spent in the tomb. That was the final Saturday Sabbath, as the next day, Sunday, God raised the body of the Christ from the tomb and instituted the Sunday Sabbath in recognition of the implementation of the indestructible Way by which men could now enter into their true rest. From resurrection Sunday forward the new Sabbath day represented the rest for which the Way was now forever *indestructible.*

Hear the words of our Lord in the book of Hebrews regarding this indestructible Way unto the true rest made available to mankind on that first Sunday Sabbath: "Now since the same promise of rest is offered to us today *(though now gloriously made available to mankind via the indestructible Way)*, let us be continually on our guard that none of us even looks like we are failing to attain it." (Heb 4:1 Phillips-ed. PBR)

And for those who think a change in the law, such as this change in the Sabbath day from Saturday to Sunday, is not possible, hear the words of our Lord, again in the book of Hebrews, where we are clearly taught that God changed the law regarding the priesthood:

"We may go further. If it be possible to bring men to spiritual maturity through the Levitical priestly system (for that is the system under which the people were given the Law), why does the necessity arise for another Priest to make His appearance after the order of Melchizedek, instead of following the normal priestly calling of Aaron? For if there is a transference of priestly powers, there will necessarily follow a change of the Law regarding priesthood. He who is described as our High Priest belongs to another tribe, no member of which had ever attended the altar! For it is a matter of history that our Lord was a descendant of Judah, and Moses made no mention of priesthood in connection with that tribe." (Heb 7:11–14 Phillips-ed. PBR)

In addition to understanding these verses as they relate to the change in the Sabbath day from Saturday to Sunday, it is also important to notice the clear distinction between the "Law" and the "Priestly System"— otherwise we might become confused and start telling ourselves that the codified Law of God from which we learn right from wrong is somehow no longer of any value.

It is important to understand that in this Epistle of Hebrews, what we see is that the Old Covenant Levitical priestly system is annulled and done away with; replaced by the New Covenant High Priest Jesus Christ! It was a transference within the overall Law, not a cancellation of the overall Law itself. Of course, when we come to this understanding, we would then expect to find the whole of the codified Law (as distinct from the Levitical priestly law embedded within it), that Law from which we learn right from wrong, still intact—and so we find it: "It can scarcely be doubted that in reality the Law itself is holy, and the commandment is holy, just and good." (Rom 7:12 Phillips-ed. PBR)

As we read further, we see more about this change within the continuing Law of the living God: "How fundamental is this change becomes all the more apparent when we see this other Priest appearing according to the Melchizedek pattern, and deriving His Priesthood not by virtue of a command imposed from outside, but from the power of indestructible life within. For the witness to Him, as we have seen, is: 'You are a priest forever according to the order of Melchizedek.'" (Heb 7:15–17 Phillips-ed. PBR)

And make note of this "indestructible life within!" for it is this that provides the true "rest." And this indestructible life within is very much connected to the change of the Sabbath day as well. And we will see as we continue our study exactly what this Indestructible Life did after leaving the cross to enable the securing of this indestructible Way for all of mankind.

Reading further we see: "Quite plainly, then, there is a definite cancellation of the previous commandment because of its ineffectiveness and uselessness—the Law was incapable of bringing anyone to real maturity and perfection *(the Levitical priestly law of the Old Covenant which has now been replaced by the new High Priest Jesus Christ, not the codified Law from which we still learn right from wrong but which never was involved in bringing 'perfection')*—followed by the introduction of a better hope, through which we approach our God. This means a 'better' hope for us because Jesus has become our Priest by the oath of God." (Heb 7:18–20 Phillips)

Indeed, it would be hard to argue that Scripture does not clearly teach of the change in the Law regarding the priesthood.

Recognizing, then, this change in the Law, now lift that

veil and come to fully understand this statement: Our
Lord Jesus Christ is *the* Lord—and the follow-up to
that: *even of the Sabbath.* In so doing, it will become
abundantly clear that God our Father, through His
Word, the visible manifestation of the triune God—
Jesus Christ, would, and did, change the Sabbath from
Saturday to Sunday. It will become evident, that along
with the change in the law whereby the priesthood was
transferred from the tribe of Levi to the person of the
Christ, we also have a change in the law connected to this
priestly transfer regarding the day of the Sabbath!

This change was and is to mark the initiation of the true
rest. This true rest coinciding with the initiation of
the better hope—the better hope being the indestructible
Way obtained by the power of that "indestructible life
within" mentioned above. The indestructible Way that
came to pass through the change in the law in relation to
our new High Priest Jesus Christ!

In Scripture, our Lord foretells of this change through His
own lips:

"And it came to pass as He went through the grain-fields
on the Sabbath day, that His disciples, as they went on
their way, began to pluck the ears. And the Pharisees
said unto Him, 'Behold, why do they on the Sabbath day,
that which is not lawful?' And He said to them, 'Have ye
never read what David did when he had need, and was an
hungered, both he, and they that were with him? How he
went into the house of God, in the days of Abiathar the
high Priest, and did eat the showbread, which were not

lawful to eat, but for the Priests, and gave also to them which were with him?' And He said to them, 'The Sabbath was made for man, and not man for the Sabbath. Wherefore the Son of man is Lord, even of the Sabbath.'" (Mark 2:23–28 GNV-ed. PBR)

We also see, in Matthew, our Lord declaring through His own lips this change in the day of the Sabbath from Saturday to Sunday:

"At that time Jesus went on a Sabbath day through the grain-fields, and His disciples were an hungered, and began to pluck the ears of grain and to eat. And when the Pharisees saw it, they said unto Him, 'Behold, thy disciples do that which is not lawful to do upon the Sabbath.' But He said unto them, 'Have ye not read what David did when he was an hungered, and they that were with him? How he entered into the house of God, and did eat the showbread, which was not lawful for him to eat, neither for them which were with him, but only for the Priests? Or have ye not read in the Law, how that on the Sabbath days the Priests in the Temple break the Sabbath, and are blameless? But I say unto you, that here is one greater than the Temple. Wherefore if ye knew what this is, I will have mercy, and not sacrifice, ye would not have condemned the innocents. For the Son of man is Lord, even of the Sabbath.'" (Mt 12:1–8 GNV-ed. PBR)

Christians, without the veil we can see that one greater than David is here! One greater than even the Old Covenant Temple! And this "great one" did as He said He would do, as our new High Priest He entered into the house of God—He was the showbread—and as our new High Priest He made the necessary changes in the law, which inured (see Glossary) to our direct benefit, including changing the day of the Sabbath from Saturday to Sunday.

Think about it like this. Did He not tell us the Sabbath was made for man, not man for the Sabbath? And now that Christ has suffered and died, descended triumphantly into Hell, proven His victory in the spiritual realm by physically rising from the dead and ascending into heaven, introducing the indestructible Way through His indestructible life, can it not be said that this Sunday Sabbath, unlike the Saturday Sabbath, "is truly made for man!" Should it not be so said? Must it not be shouted from the highest mountain and in the lowest valley, and everywhere in between?

And so it is that Christians enter into the rest of God through the change in the law regarding the priesthood *and* the day of the Sabbath. This eternal rest of God our Father through His literal Word, Jesus Christ our Lord, our indestructible Way.

The Final Preparation

Chapter Eight

"This is the book of the generation of heaven and earth, when they were made, in the day in which the Lord God *(Jesus Christ)* made the heaven and the earth." (Gn 2:4 LXX-ed. PBR)

To understand this verse, we need to recognize that the Bible is first the history book of the generation or creation of heaven and earth. Once the Bible completes this initial part of its record, it then moves on and, starting in Genesis, chapter two and verse seven, becomes the history book of the generations of Adam. And it keeps tabs throughout its record of all the sons of Adam, known in Scripture as the Nations, even all the way up to the time of the Christ.

Scripture then moves on and becomes the history book of the specific generations of the Christ through Abraham, Isaac, and Jacob. In other words, it specifically tracks the generations leading up to and including the Christ.

The Bible then records His ministry, and the implementation of the Kingdom of God; even through the Ascension and beyond. And this includes the recordation of the entrance of "man," at the Ascension, into his eternal home—heavenly paradise.

All the while the Bible maintains its historical record of the heavens and the earth, such as the world wide flood, the Tower of Babel, and the dividing of the earth during the time of Peleg.

"And every herb of the field before it was on the earth, and all the grass of the field before it sprang up, for God had not rained on the earth, and there was not a man to cultivate it." (Gn 2:5 LXX)

Before discussing this verse, recall again that on day three, when Jesus Christ created the grasses and all the vegetation, we noted that they did not yet spring forth. This was because on day three there was yet no sun, moon, or stars in the sky, and no watering of the dry land. Here in this verse, we have confirmation that this understanding of the sequence of events is correct. We also see in this verse confirmation that Jesus had not yet formed man on the earth. He had created mankind on day six, but did not form them on day six. The record in the Word is clear: "and there was not a man to cultivate it."

Then finally we see, "But there rose a fountain out of the earth, and watered the whole face of the earth." (Gn 2:6 LXX)

We have here then, the continuing progression of the fulfillment of the creation, with the triune God, after resting from the works of the creation which He *began* to do, now watering the dry land. A watering that finally brings forth the vegetation in its fully mature form across the face of the earth.

This watering also brings forth the formation in their fully mature forms all the creeping things that creep upon the earth, such as worms and insects such as ants and beetles and other bugs, etcetera, though not yet the winged flying creatures, the cattle, nor the wild beasts of the field, which we will see are formed after Adam. And this then completes the final preparation for the formation of the highest creature of all God's creation, mankind.

The Formation of Adam

Chapter Nine

"And God (*Jesus Christ*) formed the man of dust of the earth, and breathed upon his face the breath of life, and the man became a living soul." (Gn 2:7 LXX-ed. PBR)

And this living soul, Adam, was strictly and completely a part of this material world. He was not in any way a part of the spiritual world. He was made of the dust of this earth. He had blood running through the veins of his flesh. He was formed of the earth, and then became a living soul. He did not, at his formation, become a life-giving spirit.

But he did have within himself the "Way" to the spiritual dimension. He had access to the tree of life, and that access would remain so long as he remained completely obedient to the commands of God, completely in agreement with the created order of his Father. But if he were disobedient, even in any one thing, this access would be lost.

So the Way could be lost—it was not indestructible—and this destructible Way provided the framework for the initial hour of decision for Adam. And his crisis of choice was soon to come.

At this point in our study, though, let's first take a moment to understand the significance of this signal moment

within the creation—the hour of the formation of
Adam. This moment, this hour in time, is the actual
hour of decision for all the angels. Here, at the formation
of Adam, all of the angels must now make *their* choices,
for this was *their* crises of choice.

To understand why this moment is their moment in
which to choose, recall that we learned that on day six the
angels were with God when He pronounced the creation
of mankind. Try to put yourself there as the angels heard
God, through the Word Jesus Christ, speak of this final
and most magnificent creature of all His creation. Try to
imagine the feelings flowing through each of the angels as
they looked over at that uninhabited City in the Kingdom
of Light, created especially for this new creation of which
God so lovingly spoke. Consider how they must have
marveled at the care God put into this special creature.

And as the angels listened to the preaching of Jesus
Christ regarding this creation of man, they began to
understand their role. Then, there was the day of rest,
when all was good in the creation. And in that day of
rest, the angels contemplated their role within the created
order of God.

But, upon the formation of man following that first
Saturday Sabbath, when it was put upon the angels to
begin the work they were naturally created for, they had
to make a choice. Follow the Word of the Lord, serving
as nothing more than spirits in the service of God,
commissioned to serve the heirs of salvation—or rebel.

That's right, serve in God's created order as designed, or rebel against the created order and attempt to rewrite that created order after their own desires.

So this was their hour of decision, this was their crises of choice. And it was a choice that would last forever— for them there would be no second chances. Each individual of angel kind would make here for themselves an irreversible, eternal decision.

The Mutiny of Satan

Chapter Ten

Satan chose mutiny.

Of his own free will, Satan chose to blaspheme the heavenly order.

Of his own free will, Satan chose to go to war with God.

Of his own free will, Satan chose to try and implement his own way, his own "order," an adulterated order, completely foreign to the laws of nature and nature's God —Jesus Christ.

Of his own free will, Satan sought to change the interplay between the angels, God, and mankind.

So Satan fell from Grace.

Now why did Satan blaspheme the heavenly order? Why did he fall from Grace? What was the cause? Simple, really — jealous pride!

As Satan witnessed the formation of man after the day of rest, he came to the full realization of its implications. He came to understand that he would truly be but a servant to this new creation. He came to understand that this final creation would reign over even him once they entered the Kingdom of Light.

Upon the full realization of his place in the created order, Satan began his plot to overthrow the government and Kingdom of God. By his own evil pride, Satan, of his own free will, refused to accept his position as a ministering spirit to the heirs of salvation, instead choosing to blaspheme this created order and go to war with God.

You might now be thinking, "How do we know that the angels were to be spirits in the service of God, commissioned to serve the heirs of God's salvation?" In answer, hear the words of our Lord through the epistle to the Hebrews:

"For to which of the angels did He ever say such words as these: 'You are My Son, today I have begotten you?' Or, again 'I will be to Him a Father, and He shall be to Me a Son?' Further, when He brings His first-born into this world of men, He says: 'Let all the angels of God worship Him.' This is what He says of the angels: 'Who makes His angels spirits and His ministers a flame of fire.' But when He speaks of the Son, He says: 'Your throne, O God, is forever and ever; a scepter of righteousness is the scepter of Your Kingdom. You have loved righteousness and hated lawlessness; therefore God, Your God, has anointed You with the oil of gladness more than your companions.' He also says: 'You, Lord, in the beginning laid the foundation of the earth, and the heavens are the work of Your hands; they will perish, but You will remain; and they will all grow old like a garment; like a cloak You will fold them up, and they will be changed. But You are the same, and Your years will not fail.' But does He ever say this of any of the angels: 'Sit at my right hand, till I make Your enemies Your footstool?' Surely the angels are no more than spirits in the service of God, commissioned to serve the heirs of God's salvation." (Heb 1:5–14 Phillips-ed. PBR)

In plain and simple language, the Lord tells us in these verses that indeed the angels were to be servants, under God, to men, and that men would reign over them after they crossed over from this earth into heaven. And Satan's understanding of his place in the created order, and his refusal to accept such a position, was the basis of angelic sin.

To see that indeed man was to rule over the angels in heaven, let's take a look at some verses showing *the* Man who did enter heaven and now rules even over all the angels! These verses are again from the book of Hebrews:

"God, Who gave our forefathers many different glimpses of the truth in the words of the prophets, has now, in these last days, given us the truth in the Son; Whom He appointed heir of all, through Whom indeed He made the ages. This Son, radiance of the glory of God, flawless expression and express image of the nature of God, Himself the upholding principle of all that is— upholding all things by the word of His power, effected the reconciliation between God and man when He purged our sins and then took His seat at the right hand of the Majesty on high—thus proving Himself, by the more glorious name that He has won, far greater than all the angels of God." (Heb 1:1–4 Phillips-ed. PBR)

In reading further we learn as well that "For though in past ages God did grant authority to angels, yet He did not put the future world of men under their control, and it is this world that we are now talking about." (Heb 2:5 Phillips-ed. PBR)

This tells us plainly that the angels had a far greater role in the Old Testament, but that after the ascension of the Christ, that role has been diminished, as they now serve man under *the* Man, Christ Jesus.

In reading still further we learn that:

"What we actually see is Jesus, after being made temporarily inferior to the angels (and so subject to pain and death) *(tier one)*, in order that He should, in God's grace, taste death for every man, now crowned with glory and honor *(tier two)*. It was right and proper that in bringing many sons to glory, God should make the leader of their salvation, from Whom and by Whom everything exists, a perfect leader through the fact that He suffered. For the One who makes men holy and the men who are made holy share a common humanity. So that He is not ashamed to call them His brothers, for He says: 'I will declare Your name to My brethren; in the midst of the congregation I will sing praise to You.' And again, He says: 'I will put my trust in Him.' And, one more instance, in these words: 'Here am I and the children whom God has given Me.' Since, then, 'the children' have a common physical nature as partakers of flesh and blood,

He also took part of the same, so that by going through death as a man He might destroy him who had the power of death, that is, the devil; and might also set free those who lived their whole lives a prey to the fear of death *(having lost their Way from tier one to tier two)*. It is plain that for this purpose He did not become an angel; He became a man, in actual fact, a descendant of Abraham. It was imperative that He should be made like His brothers in nature, if He were to become a High Priest, both compassionate and faithful in the things of God, and at the same time, able to make propitiation for the sins of the people. For by virtue of His own suffering under temptation, He is able to help those who are exposed to temptation." (Heb 2:9–18 Phillips-ed. PBR)

From these verses, we must point out one very important point, in addition to the natural point of the angels being spirits in the service of God: In the Old Testament, according to the clear teaching of Scripture, man "lived their whole lives a prey to the fear of death;" but now, since the cross, under the New Testament, Christians live out their days without fear, as a prey to life —and eternal life at that! ("For God hath not given us the spirit of fear; but of power, and of love, and of a sound mind." [2 Tm 1:7 KJV]) This point should not be overlooked. And it is impossible to overstate. We will learn more about this as we proceed deeper into our study.

But now, back to the angels. At the time of the formation of Adam, all the angels made their one choice. Their one choice that would decide forever whether each of them individually would remain with God, or mutiny with Satan. Sadly, a full one third of the angels chose to mutiny: "And his *(Satan's)* tail drew the third part of the stars of heaven, and cast them to the earth …." (Rv 12:4 GNV-ed. PBR)

So the fall of Satan was due to his jealous pride. Satan wanted to be the highest order in the creation. Even higher than God, once he realized God's plan for mankind. He simply refused to accept his place in the created order as a ministering spirit to these heirs of salvation. Man was to rule this earth. Man was also to rule in heaven. But Satan had other plans—blaspheming the heavenly order—so Satan hatched his mutinous plan.

And the end result was that Satan was immediately cast out of heaven, as Jesus tells us: "And He *(Jesus)* said unto them, I saw Satan, like lightning, fall down from heaven." (Luke 10:18 GNV-ed. PBR) "And the great dragon was cast out, that old serpent, called the Devil, and Satan, which deceiveth the whole world: he was cast out into the earth, and his angels were cast out with him." (Rv 12:9 KJV)

Now, when Satan was cast out as described in these verses, it is important to understand to where he was cast; he was not cast out of the spiritual realm into the material realm, but he was cast out of one area of the third heaven into another. This other area of the third heaven into which he was cast is the area the Bible calls Tartarus, which, of course, was created on day one as a part of the creation of light, or the spiritual realm.

It was created for the specific purpose of holding any angels who chose of their own free will to disregard the living God, and of their own free will chose to leave His fellowship.

It was located within the bowels of the earth (remember we learned on day two that the firmament of the material heaven was stretched out throughout the entirety of the third heaven, thus the bowels of the earth would be the "lowest" point from any direction within the creation— therefore one can always refer to something or someone being cast "down" to Hell regardless of where they were within the creation or regardless of which dimension they were in).

And this place called Tartarus became the throne of Satan, where he began to plot to destroy the Way between tier one and tier two, knowing full well that if he could destroy that Way, mankind would become *his* captives. He wanted nothing less than to become a king and rule over these men which he so hated.

This is why Satan was thereafter found in the earth, and why he was in the Garden of Eden, tempting Adam and Eve. In finishing this section, read the telling words of the Lord through the prophet Isaiah regarding this prideful jealous angel, Satan, AKA Lucifer:

"How art thou fallen from heaven, O Lucifer, son of the morning! How art thou cut down to the ground, which didst weaken the nations! For thou hast said in thine heart, I will ascend into heaven, I will exalt my throne above the stars of God: I will sit also upon the mount of the congregation, in the sides of the north: I will ascend above the heights of the clouds; I will be like the most High." (Is 14:12–14 KJV-ed. PBR)

The Garden Time

Chapter Eleven

Having studied the formation of Adam, and the subsequent fall of Satan, along with the fall of a full one-third of the angels, we proceed to the next event— the placing of Adam into the Garden:

"And God *(Jesus Christ)* planted a garden eastward in Eden, and placed there the man whom He had formed. And God *(Jesus Christ)* made to spring up also out of the earth every tree beautiful to the eye and good for food, and the tree of life in the midst of the Garden, and the tree of learning the knowledge of good and evil." (Gn 2:8–9 LXX-ed. PBR)

In these verses, we have confirmed that Satan must have fallen before God places Adam in the Garden. To understand this, first recall Genesis 1:31, where we learned Satan must have fallen after day six (remember that everything on that day was still "very good"); then, recognize that from these verses here we have confirmation that he must have fallen before God places Adam into the Garden.

How so?

For upon planting the Garden, we already see within it "the tree of learning the knowledge of good and evil." And we know, as Christians with the veil already lifted, that this tree is none other than that fallen archangel, the great dragon, that old serpent, called the Devil, and Satan. So clearly Satan had already committed mutiny by the time Adam is now here placed in the Garden.

"And the Lord God *(Jesus Christ)* took the man whom He had formed, and placed him in the Garden of Delight, to cultivate and keep it. And the Lord God gave a charge to Adam, saying, 'Of every tree which is in the Garden thou mayest freely eat, but of the tree of the knowledge of good and evil—of it ye shall not eat, but in whatsoever day ye eat of it, ye shall surely die.'" (Gn 2:15–17 LXX-ed. PBR)

In these verses, we have the warning given to Adam to stay away from that fallen angel (recall the words of the Christ who did remain true to this warning, " … Get thee hence, Satan: for it is written, Thou shalt worship the Lord thy God, and Him only shalt thou serve." [Mt 4:10 KJV-ed. PBR]).

The Way unto heaven was within Adam—will Adam prove to be indestructible? We shall soon see, as the hour of decision is fast approaching for Adam—Adam will soon face his crisis of choice. But first we have the formation of Eve, to be the help mate of Adam.

"And the Lord God said, 'It is not good that the man should be alone, let us make for him a help suitable to him.'" (Gn 2:18 LXX-ed. PBR)

In this verse we come to understand God's plan for man,

as expressed in the presence of the remaining angels as once again we see this phrase "let us make," same as we saw back on day six. And this plan was that he should not be alone, but should live with a help suitable to him.

In preparation of fulfilling this plan and bringing forth the formation of a help suitable to him, God first brings before Adam all the cattle, the wild beasts of the field, and the winged flying creatures of the sky.

"And God *(Jesus Christ)* formed yet farther out of the earth all the wild beasts of the field, and all the flying creatures of the sky, and He brought them to Adam, to see what he would call them, and whatever Adam called any living creature, that was the name of it. And Adam gave names to all the cattle and to all the flying creatures of the sky, and to all the wild beasts of the field, but for Adam there was not found a help like to himself." (Gn 2:19–20 LXX-ed. PBR)

These verses provide us the actual and literal formation, by Jesus Christ, of all the winged flying creatures, and cattle, and wild beasts of the field. We see here also, the incredible intelligence of this man Adam in that he gave them all names.

By way of review, let's here summarize the order of the formation of these created beings, as the order of formation differs from the order of their creation: the living, moving creatures of the water were formed first back on day five, then after the first week of creation, the creepy crawly things such as worms and insects such as ants and beetles and other bugs of the earth—all the "creeping things that creep upon the earth" are formed at the time of the watering of the dry land, then Adam was formed upon the dry land from the very material or dust of the earth after this watering of the dry land, and then finally all the cattle and wild beasts of the field and all the winged flying creatures were formed after him.

Now among them all, there was not a help suitable to him, so then we learn that: " ... God *(Jesus Christ)* brought a trance upon Adam, and he slept, and He took one of his ribs, and filled up the flesh instead thereof. And God *(Jesus Christ)* formed the rib which He took from Adam into a woman, and brought her to Adam. And Adam said, 'This now is bone of my bones, and flesh of my flesh; she shall be called woman, because she was taken out of her husband.' Therefore shall a man leave his father and his mother and shall cleave to his wife, and they two shall be one flesh. And the two were naked, both Adam and his wife, and were not ashamed." (Gn 2:21–25 LXX-ed. PBR)

From these verses one should note that when there was just Adam and not yet any "Eve," there was obviously no means of procreation. Therefore, in order for the whole race of Adam to truly be of Adam, it was necessary for the Lord to form Eve in this peculiar way. It was only through the forming of Eve through this rib of Adam that she can be said to also come from Adam. And this is how it is that the whole of mankind can be said to come from Adam. One should also note that Adam would have been missing this rib for only a short while as this rib grows back if it is taken out. Men are not "missing" a rib due to this process of creating Eve.[5]

From these verses we also see that after naming all the cattle and all the flying creatures of the sky, and all the wild beasts of the field, the woman was formed as a help suitable to man. One man and one woman. The created order. This too cannot be overstated. In truth, any blaspheming of this created order is satanic mutiny. Fortunately, such blasphemy cannot any longer alter our indestructible Way into Heaven.

But such blasphemy can directly impact the glory of the nations, minimizing the numbers of saints a generation might produce for the Heavenly Kingdom. And should this blasphemy grow to the proportions found in Sodom and Gomorrah so long ago, then the enemies of Christ might think they can be successful in preventing any of that generation from going to Heaven. Was it not the case in Sodom and Gomorrah? That not one was found righteous?

We should also take note of the statement: "And the two were naked, both Adam and his wife, and were not ashamed." (Gn 2:25 LXX) I believe this to be a telling statement. And what I believe it to be telling us is that Adam and Eve were not directed to procreate until a certain period of testing was complete. I believe this follows from their being naked, and yet not ashamed. To me it seems reasonable to deduce that once procreation would begin, clothes would be the order of the day.

You see, nakedness today remains a part of the created design between husband and wife (even as it was with Adam and Eve, with no shame attached); but note that it is a part of the design between husband and wife *only* in their own extreme privacy. No one else is permitted to participate in that privacy. And I believe this was true in the very beginning with Adam and Eve as well. Once Adam and Eve were to bring forth children, I think it reasonable to conclude that Adam and Eve would have been introduced to clothing so as to protect their privacy —to protect their nakedness from others (see Leviticus chapter eighteen).

I believe we can further conclude that God would have given them a certain period of testing before directing them to procreate and fill the earth. Did God not build this very test into the placing of Adam into the Garden?

Now, I believe that this period of testing was forty days. I believe they were to have forty days in the Garden during which they would face the test forthcoming from Satan, that tree of learning the knowledge of good and evil. And while I understand that I am deducing certain things from the statement within the biblical account "And the two were naked, both Adam and his wife, and were not ashamed," I believe I am doing so with good reason.

For instance, we see a similar period of testing with Jesus as He also had to face forty days of testing; though we know His conditions were far from the idyllic setting of the earthly Garden of Delight. For Jesus, rather than spending forty days in the Garden of Delight, spent forty days in the wilderness. With the wild beasts. Without eating. And then was His temptation brought forth by Satan.

I think we can all recognize that the situation with Adam and Eve, when they were first placed in the Garden, is one which requires very careful consideration, for it is true that the Bible never specifically states how long Adam and Eve were in the Garden prior to their temptation and subsequent fall. So my deductions are just that, deductions garnered through an evaluation of the overall theme of the creation and the overarching story of eternal Christianity.

But they also lead to an understanding of the physical sin committed in the Garden after the mental fall to the lies of the devil. Does not Milton in *Paradise Lost* essentially conclude this very thing? And does this understanding not provide the basis for the laws regarding the redemption of the firstborn? And add value to the meaning of the virgin birth? And add value to the notion that Jesus Christ is the firstborn of every creature, of all created things? Yes indeed! And while we are born into this world through the normal means of men, we are born again into the spiritual realm, *only* through the supernatural means of Jesus Christ.

Now had Adam and Eve passed this test, they would have entered the heavenly Paradise when their appointed time on this earth was complete. Possibly through the example of Moses. Or possibly through a being taken away in a translation, similar to Enoch or the translation of Elijah. This entering into heaven would have been possible because they would not have lost their access to the spiritual Paradise, an access made available to them through the tree of life present in the Garden.

But Adam was not indestructible. Jesus was indestructible. The Son of God did come, and did pass His test. Jesus therefore obtained a much better and truly indestructible Way, and provided mankind eternal access to this tree of life.

Now a very interesting and intriguing truth to consider: It is actually a good thing that Adam and Eve failed in the Garden.

This may seem an odd statement at first, but when we understand the interplay of free will amongst the three main characters of the creation, we understand that the fall of Adam was of great benefit. Yes, in man's inevitable fall as free will beings, laid hidden the plan of the Christ!

It was through their inevitable fall that Jesus Christ would then institute indestructible access to Paradise through the tree of life for all eternity. It was through their inevitable fall that the triune God would resolve the mutinous interplay of free will throughout the creation.

And this, in the end, is the glory of the whole of the story that began even in the time before time. This is the joy of which our Lord speaks, the joy of the whole of the plan of God. This is that precious pearl. And this is the context in which we must understand the creation —and the whole of the Word of God.

The Temptation of Mankind

Chapter Twelve

At this point Adam is in the Garden along with his wife, Eve. Adam has been taught of God directly, so therefore understands the nature of the creation. Adam and Eve understand all about the first, second and third heaven. Adam and Eve understand all about the angels, their role, and that some of them had fallen.

Adam and Eve have, by our terms today, an expert level of knowledge in every subject. They are "doctors" or PhD level scholars in them all. And Adam, having the "Way" inside him to eternal life, the Way from tier one to tier two, was fully prepared to face his "temptation."

Of course, as mentioned above, this temptation is recalled when we study the temptation of the Christ, who, like Adam had forty days in which to face Satan and begin to secure that indestructible Way. We know that Jesus Christ was successful in defeating the devil. Here we will see that Adam was not.

And this fall of Adam was inevitable. And the fall led to the drama of the Christ unfolding in history. And this unfolding history was foreordained. It was built into the created plan even in the time before time—all so that beings endowed with real free will could choose their own fate—of their own accord. All so God could have eternal fellowship with those, but only those, who wanted eternal fellowship with Him. So now we pick up the story in the Garden.

"Now the serpent was the most crafty of all the brutes on the earth, which the Lord God *(Jesus Christ)* made, and the serpent said to the woman, 'Wherefore has God said, "Eat not of every tree of the Garden?"' And the woman said to the serpent, 'We may eat of the fruit of the trees of the Garden, but of the fruit of the tree which is in the midst of the Garden, God said, "Ye shall not eat of it, neither shall ye touch it, lest ye die."' And the serpent said to the woman, 'Ye shall not surely die. For God knew that in whatever day ye should eat of it your eyes would be opened, and ye would be as gods, knowing good and evil.' And the woman saw that the tree was good for food, and that it was pleasant to the eyes to look upon and beautiful to contemplate, and having taken of its fruit she ate, and she gave to her husband also with her, and they ate. And the eyes of both were opened, and they perceived that they were naked, and they sewed fig leaves together, and made themselves aprons to go round them." (Gn 3:1–7 LXX-ed. PBR)

In these verses we have the story of the actual temptation — Satan tempting Eve. And after she falls to this temptation, she then gives to her husband, who takes and eats as well.

"And the eyes of both were opened, and they perceived that they were naked, and they sewed fig leaves together, and made themselves aprons to go round them."

These words tell us quite plainly the nature of the resulting actions because of their mental acquiescence to sin.

Now I could attempt to recreate the events of that day, but why should I do that when instead, I can bring to this work a section of an epic poem considered by many scholars to be one of the greatest poems of the English language?

So, for a moment, let us reach back in time to the seventeenth century, and recall how John Milton (1608-1674), in *Paradise Lost*, imagined the events of that day. We will pick up with his work in the midst of Book IX, where we find Adam going forth to find Eve, who according to Milton, earlier in the day had persuaded Adam that they should split up so they could accomplish more of their assigned work in the Garden.

> And forth to meet her went, the way she took
> That morn when first they parted: by the tree
> Of knowledge he must pass; there he her met,
> Scarce from the tree returning; in her hand
> A bough of fairest fruit, that downy smiled,
> New gathered, and ambrosial smell diffused.
> To him she hasted; in her face excuse
> Came prologue, and apology too prompt;
> Which, with bland words at will, she thus addressed.

Hast thou not wondered, Adam, at my stay?
Thee I have missed, and thought it long, deprived
Thy presence; agony of love till now
Not felt, nor shall be twice; for never more
Mean I to try, what rash untried I sought,
The pain of absence from thy sight. But strange
Hath been the cause, and wonderful to hear:
This tree is not, as we are told, a tree
Of danger tasted, nor to evil unknown
Opening the way, but of divine effect
To open eyes, and make them Gods who taste;
And hath been tasted such: The serpent wise,
Or not restrained as we, or not obeying,
Hath eaten of the fruit; and is become,
Not dead, as we are threatened, but thenceforth
Endued with human voice and human sense,
Reasoning to admiration; and with me
Persuasively hath so prevailed, that I
Have also tasted, and have also found
The effects to correspond; opener mine eyes,
Dim erst, dilated spirits, ampler heart,
And growing up to Godhead; which for thee
Chiefly I sought, without thee can despise.
For bliss, as thou hast part, to me is bliss;
Tedious, unshared with thee, and odious soon.
Thou therefore also taste, that equal lot
May join us, equal joy, as equal love;
Lest, thou not tasting, different degree
Disjoin us, and I then too late renounce
Deity for thee, when Fate will not permit.
Thus Eve with countenance blithe her story told;
But in her cheek distemper flushing glowed.

On the other side Adam, soon as he heard
The fatal trespass done by Eve, amazed,
Astonied stood and blank, while horror chill
Ran through his veins, and all his joints relaxed;
From his slack hand the garland wreathed for Eve
Down dropt, and all the faded roses shed:
Speechless he stood and pale, till thus at length
First to himself he inward silence broke.

O fairest of Creation, last and best
Of all God's works, Creature in whom excelled
Whatever can to sight or thought be formed,
Holy, divine, good, amiable, or sweet!
How art thou lost! how on a sudden lost,
Defaced, deflowered, and now to death devote!
Rather, how hast thou yielded to transgress
The strict forbiddance, how to violate
The sacred fruit forbidden! Some cursed fraud
Of enemy hath beguiled thee, yet unknown,
And me with thee hath ruined; for with thee
Certain my resolution is to die:
How can I live without thee! how forego
Thy sweet converse, and love so dearly joined,
To live again in these wild woods forlorn!
Should God create another Eve, and I
Another rib afford, yet loss of thee
Would never from my heart: no, no!
I feel The link of Nature draw me: flesh of flesh,
Bone of my bone thou art, and from thy state
Mine never shall be parted, bliss or woe.

So having said, as one from sad dismay
Recomforted, and after thoughts disturbed
Submitting to what seemed remediless,
Thus in calm mood his words to Eve he turned.

Bold deed thou hast presumed, adventurous Eve,
And peril great provoked, who thus hast dared,
Had it been only coveting to eye
That sacred fruit, sacred to abstinence,
Much more to taste it under ban to touch.
But past who can recall, or done undo?
Not God Omnipotent, nor Fate; yet so
Perhaps thou shalt not die, perhaps the fact
Is not so heinous now, foretasted fruit,
Profaned first by the serpent, by him first
Made common, and unhallowed, ere our taste;
Nor yet on him found deadly; yet he lives;
Lives, as thou saidst, and gains to live, as Man,
Higher degree of life; inducement strong
To us, as likely tasting to attain
Proportional ascent; which cannot be
But to be Gods, or Angels, demi-Gods.
Nor can I think that God, Creator wise,
Though threatening, will in earnest so destroy
Us his prime creatures, dignified so high,
Set over all his works; which in our fall,
For us created, needs with us must fail,
Dependant made; so God shall uncreate,
Be frustrate, do, undo, and labour lose;
Not well conceived of God, who, though his power
Creation could repeat, yet would be loth
Us to abolish, lest the Adversary
Triumph, and say; "Fickle their state whom God
"Most favours; who can please him long? Me first
"He ruined, now Mankind; whom will he next?"
Matter of scorn, not to be given the Foe.

However I with thee have fixed my lot,
Certain to undergo like doom: If death
Consort with thee, death is to me as life;
So forcible within my heart I feel
The bond of Nature draw me to my own;
My own in thee, for what thou art is mine;
Our state cannot be severed; we are one,
One flesh; to lose thee were to lose myself.

So Adam; and thus Eve to him replied.
O glorious trial of exceeding love,
Illustrious evidence, example high!
Engaging me to emulate; but, short
Of thy perfection, how shall I attain,
Adam, from whose dear side I boast me sprung,
And gladly of our union hear thee speak,
One heart, one soul in both; whereof good proof
This day affords, declaring thee resolved,
Rather than death, or aught than death more dread,
Shall separate us, linked in love so dear,
To undergo with me one guilt, one crime,
If any be, of tasting this fair fruit;
Whose virtue for of good still good proceeds,
Direct, or by occasion, hath presented
This happy trial of thy love, which else
So eminently never had been known?
Were it I thought death menaced would ensue
This my attempt, I would sustain alone
The worst, and not persuade thee, rather die
Deserted, than oblige thee with a fact
Pernicious to thy peace; chiefly assured
Remarkably so late of thy so true,
So faithful, love unequalled: but I feel
Far otherwise the event; not death, but life
Augmented, opened eyes, new hopes, new joys,
Taste so divine, that what of sweet before
Hath touched my sense, flat seems to this, and harsh.
On my experience, Adam, freely taste,
And fear of death deliver to the winds.

So saying, she embraced him, and for joy
Tenderly wept; much won, that he his love
Had so ennobled, as of choice to incur
Divine displeasure for her sake, or death.

In recompence for such compliance bad
Such recompence best merits from the bough
She gave him of that fair enticing fruit
With liberal hand: he scrupled not to eat,
Against his better knowledge; not deceived,
But fondly overcome with female charm.
Earth trembled from her entrails, as again
In pangs; and Nature gave a second groan;
Sky loured; and, muttering thunder, some sad drops
Wept at completing of the mortal sin

Original: while Adam took no thought,
Eating his fill; nor Eve to iterate
Her former trespass feared, the more to sooth
Him with her loved society; that now,
As with new wine intoxicated both,
They swim in mirth, and fancy that they feel
Divinity within them breeding wings,
Wherewith to scorn the earth: But that false fruit

Far other operation first displayed,
Carnal desire inflaming; he on Eve
Began to cast lascivious eyes; she him
As wantonly repaid; in lust they burn:
Till Adam thus 'gan Eve to dalliance move.
Eve, now I see thou art exact of taste,
And elegant, of sapience no small part;
Since to each meaning savour we apply,
And palate call judicious; I the praise
Yield thee, so well this day thou hast purveyed.
Much pleasure we have lost, while we abstained
From this delightful fruit, nor known till now
True relish, tasting; if such pleasure be
In things to us forbidden, it might be wished,
For this one tree had been forbidden ten.

But come, so well refreshed, now let us play,
As meet is, after such delicious fare;
For never did thy beauty, since the day
I saw thee first and wedded thee, adorned
With all perfections, so inflame my sense
With ardour to enjoy thee, fairer now
Than ever; bounty of this virtuous tree!
So said he, and forbore not glance or toy
Of amorous intent; well understood
Of Eve, whose eye darted contagious fire.
Her hand he seised; and to a shady bank,
Thick over-head with verdant roof imbowered,
He led her nothing loth; flowers were the couch,
Pansies, and violets, and asphodel,
And hyacinth; Earth's freshest softest lap.
There they their fill of love and love's disport
Took largely, of their mutual guilt the seal,
The solace of their sin; till dewy sleep
Oppressed them, wearied with their amorous play,

Soon as the force of that fallacious fruit,
That with exhilarating vapour bland
About their spirits had played, and inmost powers
Made err, was now exhaled; and grosser sleep,
Bred of unkindly fumes, with conscious dreams
Incumbered, now had left them; up they rose
As from unrest; and, each the other viewing,
Soon found their eyes how opened, and their minds
How darkened; innocence, that as a veil
Had shadowed them from knowing ill, was gone;
Just confidence, and native righteousness,
And honour, from about them, naked left
To guilty Shame; he covered, but his robe
Uncovered more. So rose the Danite strong,
Herculean Samson, from the harlot-lap
Of Philistean Dalilah, and waked
Shorn of his strength. They destitute and bare
Of all their virtue: Silent, and in face
Confounded, long they sat, as strucken mute:
Till Adam, though not less than Eve abashed,
At length gave utterance to these words constrained.

O Eve, in evil hour thou didst give ear
To that false worm, of whomsoever taught
To counterfeit Man's voice; true in our fall,
False in our promised rising; since our eyes
Opened we find indeed, and find we know
Both good and evil; good lost, and evil got;
Bad fruit of knowledge, if this be to know;
Which leaves us naked thus, of honour void,
Of innocence, of faith, of purity,
Our wonted ornaments now soiled and stained,
And in our faces evident the signs
Of foul concupiscence; whence evil store;
Even shame, the last of evils; of the first
Be sure then.–How shall I behold the face
Henceforth of God or Angel, erst with joy
And rapture so oft beheld? Those heavenly shapes
Will dazzle now this earthly with their blaze
Insufferably bright. O! might I here
In solitude live savage; in some glade
Obscured, where highest woods, impenetrable
To star or sun-light, spread their umbrage broad
And brown as evening: Cover me, ye Pines!
Ye Cedars, with innumerable boughs
Hide me, where I may never see them more!–
But let us now, as in bad plight, devise
What best may for the present serve to hide
The parts of each from other, that seem most
To shame obnoxious, and unseemliest seen;
Some tree, whose broad smooth leaves together sewed,
And girded on our loins, may cover round
Those middle parts; that this new comer, Shame,
There sit not, and reproach us as unclean.

So counselled he, and both together went
Into the thickest wood; there soon they chose
The fig-tree; not that kind for fruit renowned,
But such as at this day, to Indians known,
In Malabar or Decan spreads her arms
Branching so broad and long, that in the ground
The bended twigs take root, and daughters grow
About the mother tree, a pillared shade
High over-arched, and echoing walks between:
There oft the Indian herdsman, shunning heat,
Shelters in cool, and tends his pasturing herds
At loop-holes cut through thickest shade: Those leaves
They gathered, broad as Amazonian targe;
And, with what skill they had, together sewed,
To gird their waist; vain covering, if to hide
Their guilt and dreaded shame! O, how unlike
To that first naked glory! Such of late
Columbus found the American, so girt
With feathered cincture; naked else, and wild
Among the trees on isles and woody shores.

Thus fenced, and, as they thought, their shame in part
Covered, but not at rest or ease of mind,
They sat them down to weep; nor only tears
Rained at their eyes, but high winds worse within
Began to rise, high passions, anger, hate,
Mistrust, suspicion, discord; and shook sore
Their inward state of mind, calm region once
And full of peace, now tost and turbulent:
For Understanding ruled not, and the Will
Heard not her lore; both in subjection now
To sensual Appetite, who from beneath
Usurping over sovran Reason claimed
Superiour sway: From thus distempered breast,
Adam, estranged in look and altered style,
Speech intermitted thus to Eve renewed.

Would thou hadst hearkened to my words, and staid
With me, as I besought thee, when that strange
Desire of wandering, this unhappy morn,
I know not whence possessed thee; we had then
Remained still happy; not, as now, despoiled
Of all our good; shamed, naked, miserable!
Let none henceforth seek needless cause to approve
The faith they owe; when earnestly they seek
Such proof, conclude, they then begin to fail.
To whom, soon moved with touch of blame, thus Eve.

What words have passed thy lips, Adam severe!
Imputest thou that to my default, or will
Of wandering, as thou callest it, which who knows
But might as ill have happened thou being by,
Or to thyself perhaps? Hadst thou been there,
Or hear the attempt, thou couldst not have discerned
Fraud in the Serpent, speaking as he spake;
No ground of enmity between us known,
Why he should mean me ill, or seek to harm.
Was I to have never parted from thy side?
As good have grown there still a lifeless rib.
Being as I am, why didst not thou, the head,
Command me absolutely not to go,
Going into such danger, as thou saidst?
Too facile then, thou didst not much gainsay;
Nay, didst permit, approve, and fair dismiss.
Hadst thou been firm and fixed in thy dissent,
Neither had I transgressed, nor thou with me.

To whom, then first incensed, Adam replied.
Is this the love, is this the recompence
Of mine to thee, ingrateful Eve! expressed
Immutable, when thou wert lost, not I;
Who might have lived, and joyed immortal bliss,
Yet willingly chose rather death with thee?
And am I now upbraided as the cause
Of thy transgressing? Not enough severe,
It seems, in thy restraint: What could I more
I warned thee, I admonished thee, foretold
The danger, and the lurking enemy
That lay in wait; beyond this, had been force;
And force upon free will hath here no place.
But confidence then bore thee on; secure
Either to meet no danger, or to find
Matter of glorious trial; and perhaps
I also erred, in overmuch admiring
What seemed in thee so perfect, that I thought
No evil durst attempt thee; but I rue
The errour now, which is become my crime,
And thou the accuser. Thus it shall befall
Him, who, to worth in women overtrusting,
Lets her will rule: restraint she will not brook;
And, left to herself, if evil thence ensue,
She first his weak indulgence will accuse.

Thus they in mutual accusation spent
The fruitless hours, but neither self-condemning;
And of their vain contest appeared no end.

Satan's Temporary Victory

Chapter Thirteen

"And they heard the voice of the Lord God *(Jesus Christ)* walking in the Garden in the afternoon; and both Adam and his wife hid themselves from the face of the Lord God *(Jesus Christ)* in the midst of the trees of the Garden." (Gn 3:8 LXX-ed. PBR)

In this verse, it seems to me that Adam and Eve were literally hiding behind Satan, as Satan was *the* tree (see Gn 3:3) "in the midst of the Garden." It also seems that this is confirmed later, as after speaking with Adam, then Eve, the Lord God Jesus Christ immediately addresses Satan.

"And the Lord God called Adam and said to him, 'Adam, where art thou?' And he said to Him, 'I heard thy voice as thou walkedst in the Garden, and I feared because I was naked and I hid myself.' And God said to him, 'Who told thee that thou wast naked, unless thou hast eaten of the tree concerning which I charged thee of it alone not to eat?' And Adam said, 'The woman whom thou gavest to be with me—she gave me of the tree and I ate.' And the Lord God said to the woman, 'Why hast thou done this?' And the woman said, 'The serpent deceived me and I ate.'" (Gn 3:9–13 LXX-ed. PBR)

Denial is such a human emotion: Adam blaming the woman; the woman blaming the serpent. But for what was the serpent to be blamed? What had Satan actually achieved that brought forth this confrontation between God and man?

Simply put, Satan had achieved the destruction of the Way, and the enslaving of mankind under himself—the prince of darkness, and the mutinous, blasphemous betrayal of free will within the creation. And all of this provided for the temporary defeat of the Kingdom of God. This was the destruction for which God came down to man in confrontation. It was all brought about by the mutinous, blasphemous interference of the devil, and the free will choice of man.

Now let's take a brief moment to understand these satanic "accomplishments." What really were the results of Adam's fall?

First, recall that Satan himself had fallen, and as a result, had been cast out of heaven, down to the earth, into the metaphysical place called Tartarus, "For if God spared not the angels that sinned, but cast them down to Tartarus … " (2 Pet 2:4 KJV-ed. PBR). (Remember we learned earlier that Tartarus is in the very center of all creation, of both realms, thus it is "down" from every location within both realms of the creation.) Upon said result of his mutiny, Satan proceeded to set up his own kingdom here on the earth, within the spiritual realm—in the place called Tartarus; within which he would then hold captive the souls of men in Hell (Hades in the Greek), another metaphysical place created in the spiritual realm right next to Tartarus.

Also recall another aspect of these two dimensions that we have previously discussed, that there is not a distance between the two dimensions in physical terms—there is instead distance only in type or kind. Now, to see an example of this, recall in Second Kings how the two dimensions are shown existing literally side by side:

"When the servant of the man of God got up early the next morning and went outside, there were troops, horses, and chariots everywhere. 'Oh, sir, what will we do now?' the young man cried to Elisha. 'Don't be afraid!' Elisha told him. 'For there are more on our side than on theirs!' Then Elisha prayed, 'O LORD, open his eyes and let him see!' The LORD opened the young man's eyes, and when he looked up, he saw that the hillside around Elisha was filled with horses and chariots of fire." (2 Kings 6:15–17 NLT)

So we see from these verses that indeed the third heaven is all about us. And thus this satanic kingdom of the third heaven was all about us as well—in fact, with its throne room right here in the bowels of the earth. And in this kingdom of Tartarus, where the prince of darkness reigned, he now would bring as captives the dead souls of fallen mankind. For mankind had lost his Way at his own fall. He had lost his Way between tier one and that Paradise in tier two. The door to enter on that Way had been closed and locked shut. Man no longer had anywhere good that he could go after his life in this physical dimension was complete.

And so he fell "down" into the bowels of the earth, into

Hell, under Satan's rule. Man would live his whole life, a prey to the fear of death. And the Prince of Darkness, Beelzebub, Lucifer, the great dragon, that old serpent, called the Devil, and Satan, was his new ruler.

And this was Satan's end game, to reign over men not only in their physical lives, but in their spiritual lives as well. And he had succeeded. Every Old Testament soul other than Enoch, Moses, and Elijah, was held captive in Hell under satanic lock and key. Thus every Old Testament soul was the prey to the fear of death, for no matter their faith and righteousness during their physical lives, they knew their immediate destiny was that they would be held captive in Hell upon their translation into tier two. And throughout the Old Testament, the fear of death among men was palpable, that haunting silent "sleep" for which the souls of those living as prey to the fear of death were destined.

So Satan held captive the souls of men in Hell upon their death as he reigned at his new home in Tartarus. He was victorious. And he was ever vigilant and on guard, forever at war with his very creator to protect his kingdom, and his reign as the prince of darkness, over these hated men.

The War in Heaven

Chapter Fourteen

"And the Lord God said to the serpent …." (Gn 3:14 LXX-ed. PBR)

The first thing to make note of from this verse is that, as we discussed previously, it appears God did not have to go and find Satan, as he was apparently right there with Adam and Eve. It does seem to me as though it was Satan behind whom they were hiding.

" … 'Because you have done this, you are yet more accursed above all cattle and all the wild beasts of the earth; on your breast and belly going forth even to consume the earth all the days of your life.'" (Gn 3:14 LXX-ed. PBR)

You see, Satan had been accursed at his own fall, but now having instigated the fall of man, he was even more so accursed. And this prophetic statement of God regarding Satan is of great import. Notice that the Lord clearly identifies for us the work of Satan—that he would go forth to consume all men, who are of course formed of the dust of the earth, all the days of his life. And this he did with a vengeance. And men are without the excuse of ignorance in falling to the lies of Satan or his children, for there can be no ignorance of this clear statement by our Lord.

"And I will put enmity between thee and the woman and between thy seed and her seed, He shall be on guard against your head, and you shall be on guard against His heel." (Gn 3:15 LXX-ed. PBR)

The Word here in Genesis 3:15 is very powerful. It explicitly foretells of the continuing progression of the great war in the third heaven begun by the mutinous rebellion of Satan. And the end of this great war.

This war in heaven was fought over the created order. It was fought over the question of who owns mankind. The war was all about the interplay of free will between the three beings so endowed; the created angelic beings, the Increate God, and created mankind.

Let's look again at this powerful verse of Genesis in paraphrase:

"And I will put enmity between thee and the woman. And between thy seed" (which are all those who are the spiritual children of Satan and follow in his mutinous blasphemous ways, ever warring against the created order of God), "and her seed" (the Christ, and all those who are born again as sons of the Christ—Christians). "He" (that is the Christ) "shall be on guard against your" (that is Satan's) "head." (That is, the Christ will be on guard against Satan converting his temporary victory over the Kingdom of God into an eternal one by being crowned as king for all eternity.) "And you" (that is Satan), "shall be on guard against His" (that is the Christ's) "heel." (That is, Satan will constantly be on guard against being crushed to death and losing his Underworld throne by the power of that great and mighty warrior, the Christ.)

Now, this war raged all throughout the Old Testament, and on into the time of the Christ—this war in heaven that was a natural and inevitable result of the triune God creating free-will beings. And this prophecy of Genesis 3:15 regarding the coming of the Christ was according to the plan of the triune God, even before the foundation of the world.

And when Jesus Christ (the visible manifestation of the invisible triune God in whom dwelt "all the fullness of God in a human body" [Col 2:9 NLT]) came and accomplished His work, He restored the Way that Adam had lost. But this time, the Way was *indestructible*!

So, at the time of the implementation of this indestructible Way, the war in heaven was essentially over. The ability for those of the metaphysical world to interfere with the Way of man was ended.

You are probably now asking yourself, "But how, specifically, was the war in heaven ended?"

The answer to this question is powerful, with implications for every aspect of your daily and eternal well being.

You see, Jesus Christ, for all intents and purposes, ended the war in heaven with His triumphant victorious battle against Satan directly after the cross. For it was Jesus

Christ the Lamb of God, who in the Spirit as that Lion of the tribe of Juda, immediately after leaving the cross that Good Friday afternoon, descended triumphantly into Hell (unlike every man before Him). So we read in First Peter: "It was in the Spirit that He transferred over and preached to the imprisoned spirits." (1 Pet 3:19 Phillips-ed. PBR)

Upon His arrival into Hell, our Lord, warring righteously for the Kingdom, immediately took hold of the dragon, that old serpent, which is the devil and Satan, and cast him bound and defeated into the bottomless pit. Then, after shutting and sealing him up, He broke down its gates.

Through His preaching He then called forth the captive saints; as He had once called forth Lazarus from the grave —even by the sound of this mighty Shepherd's own voice calling out to His lost sheep—and then celebrated His victory over the devil, with these saints, that final Saturday Sabbath—right there in the depths of Hell, in what had been their prison cells, but was now "Paradise"—as His presence filled that place.

He then provided undeniable proof of these events through the glorious demonstration of His power via the resurrection—wherein He literally rose from the grave through the bodily resurrection—and finally, the glorious Ascension, and the taking of captivity captive (the communion of the saints) to reign with Him forever in Heaven!

(As foretold in the Old Testament: "Thou hast

ascended on high, thou hast led captivity captive: thou
hast received gifts for men; yea, for the rebellious also,
that the LORD God might dwell among them." [Ps
68:18 KJV-ed. PBR] And as spoken of in the New
Testament as already fulfilled: "Wherefore He saith, When
He ascended up on high, He led captivity captive, and
gave gifts unto men." [Eph 4:8 KJV-ed. PBR])

We read in the Apostles creed this very thing:

I believe in …
Jesus Christ, His only Son, our Lord:
Who was conceived of the Holy Spirit,
born of the Virgin Mary,
suffered under Pontius Pilate,
was crucified, died, and was buried.
He descended into hell.
The third day He arose again from the dead.
He ascended into heaven
and sits at the right hand of
God the Father Almighty …
I believe in …
the communion of saints …

Can we see what a glorious and triumphant warrior is
this Jesus Christ! Look and see how this mighty warrior is
described:

"And I saw heaven open, and behold, a white horse, and
He that sat upon him was faithful and true, and in
righteousness did judge and make war. And His eyes were
as a flame of fire, and on His head were many crowns:

and He had a name written, that no man knew but Himself. And He was clothed with a garment dipped in blood, and His name is called THE WORD OF GOD. And the warriors which were in heaven followed Him upon white horses, clothed with fine linen white and pure. And out of His mouth went out a sharp sword, that with it He should smite the heathen: and He shall rule them with a rod of iron: and He it is that treadeth the wine press of the fierceness and wrath of almighty God. And He hath upon His garment, and upon His thigh a name written, THE KING OF KINGS, AND LORD OF LORDS." (Rv 19:11–16 Tyndale-ed. PBR)

So the war in heaven is for all intents and purposes, over.

And what remains yet today is not a war in heaven, for Jesus Christ has defeated Satan's ability to ever again disrupt man's Way into Heaven. No, the only thing that remains is the war on earth.

The natural war amongst mankind.

The war between those of mankind who are of the seed of Christ and those of mankind who are of the " … seed of Satan." (see Rv 2:9) Between those who, of their own free will, choose fellowship with God our Father through the Lord Jesus Christ, and those of mankind who of their own free will choose the fellowship of the blasphemous satanic path of rebellious mutiny against Jesus Christ and the created order of the triune God.

The war between eternal Christendom and the multitudinous anti-Christ—the heathen.

The very real war determining within each and every generation the numbers of saints supplied to the ever growing Kingdom of the Living God.

Our Present Triumphant State

Chapter Fifteen

"And to the woman He said, 'I will greatly multiply your pains and your groanings; in pain you will bring forth children, and your submission shall be to your husband, and he shall rule over you.'" (Gn 3:16 LXX-ed. PBR)

In these verses we have the clear statement by God that as originally designed, there was in the natural law, discomfort associated with childbirth, but that after the fall that pain was greatly increased and multiplied.

We also have the clear direction for family life, that the wife will continue to give regard to her husband, thus casting in stone the pre-fall or "Garden of Eden pre-sin" patriarchal order of the true Christian family.

And while this patriarchal order remains true even today, it is not to be confused with a lack of equality before the Throne of God. The created order of God includes many different levels in the chain of command within His Kingdom, all for the benefit of the continuing participants. There is no communism or egalitarianism (see Glossary) to be found in the created order of the Kingdom (see 1 Cor 12:14–26). But there is an absolute equality of redemption and salvation for all of mankind, both man and woman.

And this is why throughout history, Christianity has

always recognized both the natural created order, and the equality one to another of both the mate and the help mate. In the created order: there are differences in roles, and responsibilities, and relationships. Before the throne: there is exact equality—neither man nor woman is better, neither one is before the other, but they are together as one.

"And to Adam He said, 'Because you have hearkened to the voice of your wife, and eaten of the tree concerning which I charged you of it only not to eat—of that thou hast eaten, cursed is the ground in your labors, in pain will you eat of it all the days of your life. Thorns and thistles shall it bring forth to you, and you will eat the herb of the field. In the sweat of your face shall you eat your bread until you return to the earth out of which you were taken, for earth you are and to earth you shall return.'" (Gn 3:17–19 LXX-ed. PBR)

Thorns and thistles are not here a new creation, they were always a part of the original creation; it is just that now, outside of the Garden of Delight, Adam would have to contend with these thorns and thistles as a part of his husbandry.

But this hard work has become known in the New Testament, to all those of steadfast Christian maturity —as but a pleasant gift of sweet maturation toward Paradise.

And what a pleasant gift it is, for what a perfect situation we find ourselves in since the Theophany (the visible manifestation of the invisible God through the Incarnation as Jesus Christ—"a visible manifestation of a deity"—see Glossary) and the implementation of the indestructible Way. For we now have opportunity here in this earthly "birthing center" to work and labor, and by faith, obtain eternal life through Christ. After which we will enter Paradise and live forever!

And this Way is indestructible. And this Way is perfect, because as Christians we can no longer sin unto death, for even when we fall to sin we are still washed in the blood of Christ.

So, when we pass from this life to the next, and stand before that throne of the living God upon which Jesus Christ sits, as He is the One who is the visible expression of the invisible God, " ... then shall be brought to pass the saying that is written: 'Death is swallowed up in victory.' 'O death, where is your victory? O death, where is your sting?'" (1 Cor 15:54–55 KJV-ed. PBR)

"And Adam called the name of his wife Eve, because she was the mother of all living. And the Lord God *(Jesus Christ)* made for Adam and his wife garments of skin, and clothed them. And God said, 'Behold, Adam is become as one of us, to know good and evil, and now lest at any time he stretch forth his hand, and take of the tree of life and eat, and so he shall live forever'—So the Lord God sent him forth out of the Garden of Delight to cultivate the ground out of which he was taken. And He cast out Adam and caused him to dwell over against the Garden of Delight, and stationed the cherubs and the fiery sword that turns about to keep the way of the tree of life." (Gn 3:20–24 LXX-ed. PBR)

In these verses, we see again that God was speaking in the presence of the angels. And that Adam and Eve were given clothes of animal skin by the Lord, in essence confirming that the Lord had built into the creation the means by which Adam and Eve would ultimately be clothed, sin or no.

Then we see, after having been clothed by God to protect their marital privacy and re-establish clothing's original intent and proper purpose, they are cast out of the Garden of Delight—never to return. And this casting out was a part of the glorious, but at the time hidden, foreordained plan of the triune God.

We see also the guardians stationed to keep the Way of the tree of life. And we should make note that these guardians were of the third heaven, of the metaphysical world, of that Kingdom of Light. Why were they of the spiritual dimension? *Because this was, and is yet today, the realm of true Paradise.*

And in this Kingdom of Light, as they stood watch, these guardians were to "keep the Way" until a worthy one approached. And keep the Way they did, for thousands of years, until one day, many years ago, a certain Man approached; a Man clothed with a garment dipped in blood.

And as this Man approached, these cherubs fell to their knees, and the fiery sword stilled, and the Man walked through that door—and the Way was opened.

And since that time, the blessed labor of our earthly physical life unto which Adam was once cast, but to which we are now called, teaches us the blessed faith by which we now enter into Paradise.

Conclusion

After reading this book, my fondest hope is that you now plainly see the Gospel of Jesus Christ, even as it existed in the time before time, even before the foundation of the world—including the plan of God; the actualization of this plan through the visible manifestation of the triune God, the Word made flesh; and the *hope* of this plan now implemented through that indestructible life of Jesus Christ.

" ... Now the Son of God came to earth with the express purpose of undoing the works of the devil."
(1 Jn 3:8 Phillips-ed. PBR)

The result of such a *triumphant* viewpoint is a worldview, and a heavenview, that includes an overwhelming consciousness of the victory of Jesus Christ. And this triumphant world-and-heaven view is, simply put, the "good news" of the Gospel of Jesus Christ, the good news of the Gospel of the Kingdom.

As you go forward, consider carrying this triumph of hope in your heart, this triumph of the Kingdom of God, and allowing the motion of the Spirit to amend your life more and more toward the created order of Jesus Christ.

For there is no greater gift to beings endowed with free will, than the invitation to Paradise through the indestructible Way. And there is no greater response, but to accept this invitation to sup at the table of our Lord.

"The greatest demonstration of God's love for us
has been His sending His Son, the Only-Begotten,
into the world, to give us life through Him.
We see real love, not in the fact that we loved God,
but that He loved us and sent His Son to be the
propitiation for our sins."
(1 Jn 4:9–10 Phillips-ed. PBR)

And in so doing, the glory of the nations will increase, the angels will rejoice, and Jesus Christ will magnify the celebration of the reconciliation of the earth through the ever increasing expansion of His eternal Kingdom.

Cherish the Gospel, that precious pearl for which we should sell everything (rid ourselves of all our human pride), all that we have (remember Satan's jealous pride), in order that we might obtain unto its glory.

And remember, "Without faith, it is impossible to please Him. The man who approaches God must have faith in two things—first, that God exists, and second, that it is worth a man's while to try to find God." (Heb 11:6 Phillips-ed. PBR)

May our Lord and our God, Jesus Christ, bless and keep us all in His amazing love.

Afterword

I want to take just a moment and thank you for reading this book—I truly hope you found it helpful.

I also want to encourage you to continue on in your spiritual journey. In this light, I have put together a Daily Bible Reading Program—with pastoral teaching through numerous footnotes—that makes it easy for you and your family to regularly spend quality time in the Word.

Trusting that moving past the basics of salvation into the depth of the faith is how we best engage our own souls and those of our young people, this Daily Bible Reading Program was created to make it as easy as possible for you and your family to walk daily in His Word.

You see, I believe that with prayer and a regular commitment to reading the Word, we can see our selves and our young people fully commit to the royal faith. By spending time daily in the Word, I believe we can all come to know ever more deeply the wondrous glory of Jesus Christ, and thus grow into spiritual maturity.

In closing, please accept my invitation to share any thoughts or feedback you might have—you can email me at info@cjrpress.com.

I also invite you to learn more about the Daily Bible Reading Program at www.spiritualfitnessprogram.com.

You will find that, like this book, it consistently presents from a triumphant viewpoint the depth of the gospel message of Jesus Christ and the full good news of His Kingdom.

Our continuing mission with this additional tool for supporting disciple's of Christ and their walk with Him is simple, to help further enable you and your family to live a more powerful and victorious Christian life—and thus to help your family successfully pass on the faith from generation to generation.

I wish you well in your walk of faith, and that you find yourself always growing in your personal relationship with Jesus Christ—the triumphant King of Kings and Lord of Lords.

About the Author

Paul has been studying and reading the Bible for over 30 years. With that experience came the passion to help fellow Christians go from casual Christianity to active and sustainable Christianity.

Driven by that passion, Paul developed the Essential Spiritual Fitness Program, the simple yet proven method to help every Christian grow beyond the good news of salvation into the fullness of the Kingdom.

Outside of helping disciples of Christ actively apply His teachings, Paul continues his career in the business world leading high performance teams. All the while, raising his family and writing books on our faith and its practical application in the real world.

Abbreviations

Amos *or* Am	Amos
1 Chron. *or* 1 Chr	1 Chronicles
2 Chron. *or* 2 Chr	2 Chronicles
Dan. *or* Dn	Daniel
Deut. *or* Dt	Deuteronomy
Eccles. *or* Eccl	Ecclesiastes
Esther *or* Est	Esther
Exod. *or* Ex	Exodus
Ezek. *or* Ez	Ezekiel
Ezra *or* Ezr	Ezra
Gen. *or* Gn	Genesis
Hab. *or* Hb	Habakkuk
Hag. *or* Hg	Haggai
Hosea *or* Hos	Hosea
Isa. *or* Is	Isaiah
Jer. *or* Jer	Jeremiah
Job *or* Jb	Job
Joel *or* Jl	Joel
Jon. *or* Jon	Jonah
Josh. *or* Jo	Joshua
Judg. *or* Jgs	Judges
1 Kings *or* 1 Kgs	1 Kings
2 Kings *or* 2 Kgs	2 Kings
Lam. *or* Lam	Lamentations
Lev. *or* Lv	Leviticus
Mal. *or* Mal	Malachi
Mic. *or* Mi	Micah
Nah. *or* Na	Nahum
Neh. *or* Neh	Nehemiah
Num. *or* Nm	Numbers
Obad. *or* Ob	Obadiah
Prov. *or* Prv	Proverbs
Ps. (*pl.* Pss.) *or* Ps (*pl.* Pss)	Psalms
Ruth *or* Ru	Ruth
1 Sam. *or* 1 Sm	1 Samuel
2 Sam. *or* 2 Sm	2 Samuel
Song of Sol. *or* Sg	Song of Solomon (= Song of

Songs)

| Zech. *or* Zec | Zechariah |
| Zeph. *or* Zep | Zephaniah |

Additions to Esther (= The Rest of Esther)

Bar. *or* Bar — Baruch
Bel and Dragon — Bel and the Dragon
Ecclus. — Ecclesiasticus (= Sirach)
1 Esd. — 1 Esdras
2 Esd. — 2 Esdras
Jth. *or* Jdt — Judith
1 Macc. *or* 1 Mc — 1 Maccabees
2 Macc. *or* 2 Mc — 2 Maccabees
Pr. of Man. — Prayer of Manasses (= Manasseh)

Sir — Sirach (= Ecclesiasticus)

Song of Three Children — Song of the Three Holy Children

Sus. — Susanna
Rest of Esther — (= Additions to Esther)

Tob. *or* Tb — Tobit
Ws — Wisdom (= Wisdom of Solomon)

Wisd. of Sol. — Wisdom of Solomon (= Wisdom)

Acts	Acts of the Apostles
Apoc. (= Revelation)	Apocalypse
Col. *or* Col	Colossians
1 Cor. *or* 1 Cor	1 Corinthians
2 Cor. *or* 2 Cor	2 Corinthians
Eph. *or* Eph	Ephesians
Gal. *or* Gal	Galatians
Heb. *or* Heb	Hebrews
James *or* Jas	James
John *or* Jn	John (Gospel)
1 John *or* 1 Jn	1 John (Epistle)
2 John *or* 2 Jn	2 John (Epistle)
3 John *or* 3 Jn	3 John (Epistle)
Jude	Jude
Luke *or* Lk	Luke
Mark *or* Mk	Mark
Matt. *or* Mt	Matthew
1 Pet. *or* 1 Pt	1 Peter
2 Pet. *or* 2 Pt	2 Peter
Phil. *or* Phil	Philippians
Philem. *or* Phlm	Philemon
Rev. *or* Rv (= Apocalypse)	Revelation
Rom. *or* Rom	Romans
1 Thess. *or* 1 Thes	1 Thessalonians
2 Thess. *or* 2 Thes	2 Thessalonians
1 Tim. *or* 1 Tm	1 Timothy
2 Tim. *or* 2 Tm	2 Timothy
Titus *or* Ti	Titus

GNV	Geneva Bible (1599), edited by Paul B. Rakowicz
KJV	King James Version
LXX	Septuagint
NLT	New Living Translation
Phillips	J.B. Phillips, "The New Testament in Modern English," 1962
Tyndale	Tyndale New Testament 1534
ed. PBR	A compilation of the biblical text based on the text of the stated source, addressing punctuation, capitalization, and word choice to improve ease-of-reading and ease-of-understanding

Glossary

Source: Merriam-Webster's Collegiate Dictionary, 4ᵗʰ ed. (Merriam-Webster, Incorporated. Springfield, Massachusetts, U.S.A., 2008)

egalitarian. Asserting, promoting, or marked by egalitarianism.

egalitarianism. (1): A belief in human equality especially with respect to social, political, and economic rights and privileges (2): A social philosophy advocating the removal of inequalities among people.

ex nihilo. From out of nothing.

fiat. (1): A command or act of will that creates something without or as if without further effort (2): An authoritative determination: Dictate (3): An authoritative or arbitrary order: Decree.

increate. Uncreated.

inscrutable. Not readily investigated, interpreted, or understood.

inure. To become of advantage.

primer. (3): A short, informative piece of writing.

sublime. (1): To elevate or exalt especially in dignity or honor (2): To render finer (as in purity or excellence).

theophany. A visible manifestation of a deity.

Notes

1. Jaroslav Pelikan, *Whose Bible Is It?: A Short History of the Scriptures* (New York: Penguin, 2006), 198

2. Sir Lancelot C.L. Brenton, *The Septuagint with Apocrypha: Greek and English* (Hendrickson Publishers. Originally published by Samuel Bagster & Sons, Ltd., London, 1851.)

3. Arthur M. Ogden, *The Development of the New Testament* (Ogden Publications. 2nd Edition. Revised. 1995.)

4. There are many who believe that "into" of verse 42 should be "in." I am comfortable with either word, given that in the very next verse Jesus says, "Today shalt thou be with me in Paradise," and one is therefore left with the clear impression that Jesus was speaking of that very day, that very Friday afternoon, and therefore the "into" or "in" both have really to fit within the framework of the "today" of that next verse—verse 43.

5. Bania MA, Negrin JA. *Scintigraphic Evidence of Post-surgical Rib Regrowth* (Clin. Nucl. Med. 1995 Feb; 20 (2): 185–186. North Shore University Hospital, Division of Nuclear Medicine, Manhasset, NY 11030, U.S.A., http://www.ncbi.nlm.nih.gov/sites/entrez

Made in the USA
Columbia, SC
16 September 2017